D0450699

A New Beginning:

Stories of Recovery from Relapse

A New Beginning:

Stories of Recovery from Relapse

OVEREATERS
ANONYMOUS®

Overeaters Anonymous, Inc.

A New Beginning:

Stories of Recovery from Relapse

Rio Rancho, New Mexico

ISBN 1-889681-01-6

Library of Congress Catalog Card No.: 97-76416

Overeaters Anonymous, Inc.

World Service Office

6075 Zenith Court NE

Rio Rancho, New Mexico 87144-6424 USA

Mailing address: P.O. Box 44020

Rio Rancho, NM 87174-4020 USA

(505) 891-2664

www.oa.org

PREFACE

This book is a collection of stories and essays on the topic of recovery from relapse. All were written by members of the Overeaters Anonymous Fellowship and were published between 1991 and 1996 in *Lifeline*, OA's monthly magazine. The opinions expressed are those of the individual writers and do not represent OA as a whole. Their words are not intended to give definitive or ideological answers to questions about recovery from relapse; rather, they represent many different examples of experience, strength, and hope.

Whether you are a long-timer struggling with abstinence, a newcomer for whom the topic of relapse and recovery may still be a mystery, or a member wishing to be of service to relapsing OA members, may you find encouragement in these pages.

TABLE OF CONTENTS

Chapter Three: *"My love and prayers surround you ..."*
How can abstinent OAers help still-struggling members?

Chapter Four: *"I choose to continue in this program. . ."*
A surrender to OA's simple program renewed these members' abstinence.

Chapter Five: *"I know now why I relapsed ..."*
Members share the lessons they learned during their relapse experiences.

FOREWORD

A Zest for Living *By Rozanne S., OA's cofounder*

A new day was beginning. The early morning sky was blue; the breeze fresh and crisp. Suddenly my phone rang.

"Oh, Rozanne!" the caller cried. "What shall I do? I've been in and out of OA for twelve years, but I only have one foot in the OA door. Meetings are so boring; eating plans are confusing. I still have to lose twenty pounds, but I don't seem to be able to do it. I'm not really happy inside. How do you maintain your enthusiasm about OA and the program?"

How indeed. This was a serious, thought-provoking question. What happens to us after we've been in OA for a period of time? Is inventory-taking becoming too much trouble? Does our prayer and meditation time grow stale? Is our carefully crafted food plan turning into the same old thing each day? Is it easier to go to a movie than to a meeting? Do the speakers all begin to sound alike?

Sometimes we find ourselves resting on our laurels. Maybe we've been at a normal weight for quite awhile. Family relations may be smoother. Our job situation is finally stable. The threat to our health from overweight is diminishing. We no longer overreact to every little thing. OA becomes one same old happening after another.

What happened to that pink cloud feeling we had as newcomers? It was so exciting; everything was new and hopeful. Recovery could be ours! Where did that euphoria go?

Perhaps we can't maintain that ecstatic newness forever, but we can find something even better – a joyous appreciation of life without excess food.

What steps can we take to maintain a zest for living no matter how long we've been in OA, no matter what life throws at us?

First we must remember what it was like during the depths of our overeating. Hopelessness and despair were our constant companions. Frustration and rage overwhelmed us. Life scarcely seemed worth living.

Next we must realize that, with God's help, our dark past is our greatest possession – the key to maintaining our own happiness while bringing joy and peace of mind to others. We must share our experience and talk about our recovery honestly. Let's give other overeaters hope that, if recovery happened to us, it can happen to them.

Each day we make an effort to "act as if." As we go about our daily activities, we smile. When someone asks, "How are you?" we answer, "Fine." This is not intended as a denial of our feelings. Rather the very act of affirming we are okay banishes self-pity and makes us feel better. A positive life becomes reality.

This doesn't eliminate the need for inventories, for clearing away the wreckage of the past and sweeping up the emotional debris of the present. What this attitude does engender is the feeling of "my glass is half-full" instead of "what's the use – my glass is half-empty."

Most important of all, before rushing into each new day, let's center ourselves with the Higher Power of our choice. According to the Third Step, we make a decision to turn our lives and our wills over to the care of God as we understand God. What a relief!

Now we can relax and enjoy life.

In the end that attitude is what this program is all about. During my initial recovery thirty-one years ago, two later relapses and my current recovery in OA, I learned that life doesn't have to be full of tears. I don't have to be a victim of my past. I can take responsibility for my present and approach my future with anticipation and excitement.

I can be gentle with myself where my feelings are concerned and firm with myself when it comes to my daily food intake. Being at a normal weight is terrific; enjoying life each day is a positive challenge.

Recovery is a journey, not a destination. Let's take that trip together. The "Road of Happy Destiny" mentioned in the "Big Book" can be trudged, but it can also be walked, skipped and run.

How do you want to live the rest of your life? The choice is yours.

"I knew I was in danger..."

Recognizing the warning signs of relapse
can help members maintain abstinence.
Failure to take action can lead to relapse.

A Child's Poem

I was returning home from dropping off some departing guests at the airport when I realized that I was dangerously tired. I anticipated a hard night. Meanwhile, my eleven-year-old daughter and her cousin decided to go to a movie.

"Ah ha!" I thought, as a light went on in my head, "I will be all alone. I can binge."

> That night, my Higher Power spoke to me through the words of my precious eleven-year-old child.

On the way to drop the girls at the movie, I planned my binge. I was irritable and jumpy. I couldn't wait to be alone. I dropped the girls off and was on my way for a sugar high. I rationalized that I would do it this once and then stop. I would then start off tomorrow "right," but just now I felt I was at the point of no return.

About a minute before I was to turn in at the store, my daughter entered my thoughts. Our relationship has really grown in my years of recovery, and she continues to be a real support.

A poem she had recently written came into my mind. I was flooded with the awareness of her disappointment in me if I were to lose my abstinence that night.

The lines of her poem ran through my mind: "When you eat one, you want one more, then two, then three, then pretty soon, four."

Flooded with emotion, I passed the store without stopping.

You see, my daughter takes my disease very seriously. I've been hospitalized twice, once for complications from overeating and once again to treat the problem. She knows that this disease is cunning, baffling, and powerful. She also believes it can be fatal.

When I got home, I took the poem out of my wallet where I keep it and read the last line: "Without these foods, it may seem lame, but without you, it wouldn't be the same."

I stood out in the yard and looked up at the swaying cedar trees. Tears started running down my face. I walked inside and made a phone call to an OA friend.

I also believe this disease is powerful and, if left unchecked, fatal. That night, my Higher Power spoke to me through the words of my precious eleven-year-old child. Thank you, HP, for granting me the willingness to listen.

— *Washington USA*

Change of Tune

As a member of a touring company of musicians, I was playing one dark November evening in a castle outside of Munich, Germany. All decisions about meals, travel, and accommodations had been taken completely out of our hands by the tour's organizers, and I'd been finding it harder and harder to plan my meals due to the disorganization of the tour.

I was feeling very shaky and had gone off to find some privacy to tune my instrument and to pray. My solitude was interrupted by some of the others, informing me that the evening meal before the concert had been cancelled. We'd have to wait until afterwards – if we could find a restaurant that was still open.

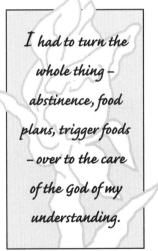

I had to turn the whole thing – abstinence, food plans, trigger foods – over to the care of the God of my understanding.

After a week of similar occurrences, this was too much for me. My eating plan in ruins, I burst into tears. After an emotional discussion, the organizer acknowledged my need to be able to plan my daily food and agreed to try to do better in the weeks remaining.

That night I crossed a line. I'd been brought to a point of no choice. I had to turn the whole thing – abstinence, food plans, trigger foods – over to the care of the God of my understanding.

On the spot, I redefined my plan of eating for the remainder of the trip as 3-0-1: three moderate meals and no snacks each day. I gave up worrying about what I ate and when. Since I couldn't call anyone back home, I wrote an OA friend about my decision.

I'd brought my Region Nine meeting directory with me, but after several wrong numbers, coupled with the fact that I don't speak German, I'd given up trying to make contact with another OA in Germany, or getting to a meeting anywhere within a few hours drive of the part of Bavaria I was in.

The tour eventually ended, and I returned home to England where I've lived for the past ten years. I was exhausted, and I still had the Christmas season face. But I want to share the results of that day in Munich.

In January, when I went to my regular monthly weigh-in, I discovered that I had lost three and a half pounds – even though I'd done nothing except turn my food over and eat three meals each day.

This experience has given me great hope, an assurance that the program works, and the conviction that the God of my understanding looks after me even when I can't look after myself.

— *England*

False Evidence Appearing Real

The weekend had been hard. The obsession with food had returned. I found myself wanting to break my abstinence and only half-caring whether I did so. I wanted more.

I found myself not calling in my food to my sponsor, ignoring my meditation books, ignoring my program. I wondered, "How did it get so bad so fast?" I wanted to know why.

My life had seemed to be in order, without impending crises. The only things bugging me were tragedies happening to several people I knew. I couldn't understand why I was being bowled over by something not affecting me personally, and I tried to find other causes for my emotional distress. I couldn't.

OA has taught me to turn and face my fears. I've learned that fear underlies much of my compulsive overeating, and I've learned if I don't face my fears, they will drive me to bingeing again. I knew I was in a dangerous place and knew I needed to act immediately. I began using the Steps and the tools that had worked for me in the past:

- Got in touch with my Higher Power and admitted my powerlessness over the food and my fears.
- Called my sponsor, committed my food for the day, and informed her of the bad spot I was in.
- Committed to my sponsor to write in my journal about my feelings.
- Went to an OA meeting, listened, and shared with fellow members.
- Wrote in my journal the next morning.
- Shared the results of my journal writing with my sponsor and another member.

The results of my writing were a shock to me. I asked myself why I was scared and why bad things happen to good people. I decided that I was healthier now and could bear more. Yet my conclusion was: "I'm going to go back to the food so I won't have to cope with more, and I can protect those I love from tragedy."

This, of course, was stinking thinking in the extreme. I was appalled at where my emotions had led. No wonder I felt so scared! The logic behind this felt real, but of course wasn't. It was False Evidence Appearing Real. But this fear couldn't stand the light of day. It could only exist when its "logic" was hidden from my consciousness. My journal writing lifted my obsession with food again.

My abstinence has granted me access to my emotions. It's truly the most important thing in my life. It takes all of the tools of the program working together to keep me abstinent.

Thank you, OA, for the Steps, my fellow members, and the tools. They work if you work them.

— *Indiana USA*

Honesty, Trust, and Action

After reading articles on honesty in *Lifeline*, I was jolted out of complacency into action in a big way. I had been having a long dry spell with my program, and, being a relative newcomer, didn't know what to do. I wasn't at the point where I could really trust others in the program, my sponsor, or my unworkable concept of how my Higher Power was to help me out of my difficulty. I had been neglecting my reading and my sponsor. I had made a commitment to call in my food to an OA woman in my area but didn't call her for eight weeks. I had rationalized that commitments were hard for me, and telling another person what I was actually eating was far too personal. Anyway I didn't think I was doing too badly. Until I read the articles in *Lifeline*.

> *Without honesty, I have no foundation upon which to build, and my program collapses under its own weight and the weight of my urges toward control and self-will.*

I suddenly realized that my problems stemmed from a lack of action, a lack of trust, and a lack of honesty about all three aspects of my program. I had been adrift for a long time, not having a good concept of what my Higher Power was and mystified about the emotional and spiritual aspects of the program. I had read that this was a three-fold program, but I could only relate to the physical part, having had some physical recovery since I began this program last October. That all changed after reading about honesty in *Lifeline*. I knew then that lack of honesty and lack of action on my part were at the root of my troubles.

So I took the advice of my sponsor and went back to *The Twelve-Step Workbook of Overeaters Anonymous* and answered the questions in Steps One, Two, and Three again, especially the ones centering around expectations of what my Higher Power is and what my Higher Power can do for me. With much fear of my old God, I sat down and wrote a description of what I really want and need from a Higher Power and decided to act as if I could act as if. What I found was amazing. When I honestly laid out my fears and expectations, I found that I could actually visualize this Power, and I knew somehow that it had been an integral part of myself all along. My old concept of God wasn't working, but I was terrified to change my way of thinking about God lest the hand of this terrible imagined almighty smite me down in my tracks for such blasphemy.

When I wrote my description of what I really need, it came to me that a loving God would surely rather I have a flawed concept that would allow some channel of communication, however imperfect, instead of having an unworkable one that fostered fear and distrust and no communication at all. I had to step out with blind faith, act as if, and do it anyway. And it worked! Since then, I have made it a habit to visualize my Higher Power often and to actually ask for guidance. I find that I'm getting answers for the first time in my thirty-two years on earth.

I also made a commitment to myself and to my sponsors that I would ask myself the following questions about this three-fold program every day and answer them with absolute honesty.

Physical: How is your abstinence? Were there any items on your "not allowed" list that you indulged in today? My new watchword is, "If it is not on my abstinence list, don't eat it, no matter what." This takes away any decision and lessens my conflicting emotions surrounding eating. Eating then becomes nourishment for my body and nothing more. There is no room for rationalization or excuses, and no opportunity to slip.

Emotional: How are you handling your feelings? Are you even having feelings? How is your emotional health? I must exist in this moment, which, good or bad, will pass. If I choose to ignore my reactions, feelings, and emotions, I'm not being honest. I can't control my feelings or my emotions, but I can choose my course of action and how I handle those feelings.

Spiritual: How is your spiritual program? Are you comfortable with your concept of a Higher Power, and is it working for you? Do you communicate with your Higher Power? Most important of all, do you trust it? I tried to analyze this portion of my program and found that I cannot. Faith, especially for a nonreligious person like me, must simply be experienced. Faith for me is not a gift. I have to just do it and work at it every day. My Higher Power doesn't dump things ready-made into my lap, so I meet my Higher Power halfway by practicing my faith. I must. It's the only thing keeping me alive and in this program.

Action: This is a program of action. What action did you take today for your recovery and toward your life goals? Recovery from this disease will not be handed to me on a silver platter. I have to work at it every day. I make a daily commitment to my sponsors to take responsibility for myself and to take some action, however small it might be, in the direction of recovery. I write, I read, I call, or I take action, one Step at a time, one moment at a time. Even the smallest action has tremendous power.

When I am not honest with myself or others, I have no spiritual connections; my life is dead. Without honesty, I avoid my emotions and try to stifle feelings of unpleasantness and even great joy, two things I'm uncomfortable with. Without honesty, I have no physical recovery, especially when I lie to my sponsors and omit telling them about foods that I have eaten and slips I've made, or when I lie about any other part of my program. Honesty is an integral ingredient of all three aspects of the program for me. Without it I have no foundation upon which to build, and my program collapses under its own weight and the weight of my urges toward control and self-will.

Playing around with my food, hiding my feelings, having no trust in a Higher Power, and doing nothing put me on the slippery ramp which I call the black spiral into despair and chaos. Working the Steps, using the tools, taking action, asking for guidance from my Higher Power, and being honest keep me loving life and recovering.

I hope that sharing this experience, strength, and hope will be what someone else needs to hear. I certainly heard what I needed. What was freely given to me, I give to you.

— *Alabama USA*

Side Dish

"One hot summer night," writes a member from Washington, D.C., "I was sitting on the front stoop of my house debating whether or not I could 'handle' an ice cream cone. At that moment, a truck drove past with the letters 'G.O.D.' written on its side. Never mind that the letters really stood for 'General Office Delivery,' I knew what they meant for me!"

Weakness, Not Strength

I recently came to a deeper understanding of that phrase used in the introduction in many meetings: "It is our weakness, not strength, which brings us together." I usually squirmed at the notion of weakness, and though I could admit to being weak at the sight of food, I didn't like to be reminded of it.

But recently my Higher Power taught me a rich and gentle lesson about what weakness means for me in OA. At work I was having a very difficult time with a certain project. I even applied for another job, hoping life would be more serene somewhere else, but something in me suggested that I should just ask for help rather than jump ship. So, contrary to my usual display of "togetherness," I let my manager in on my feelings. I shared my lack of confidence, and when I told him how he could help, he said he would. Wow.

I presented myself as being in need of help instead of having it all together.

Soon I had to grapple with my school courses and make arrangements for the following quarter. I asked a faculty member, whom I had only met once, for help. He said he could. Hmm.

Then I finally noticed that my food was shaky during this time. I called an OA member from my meeting who seemed quite serene; I asked her if she would help me analyze my food habits and make any suggestions that seemed appropriate. She said yes. Okay.

By then I realized my Higher Power was doing for me what I could not do for myself. In each of these situations I presented myself as being in need of help instead of having it all together (Step One); I realized that I could not do it alone and that there was a Power greater than myself who could help (Step Two); and I decided to ask that Power, in the form of other people, for help (Step Three).

Thank you, Higher Power, for the awareness that you always find ways to give me what I need.

— *Washington USA*

My Spiritual Barometer

I've been in the OA program since July 1990, and I've heard many times that when we are slipping "the food is the last to go." This is both true and not true in my program. For me, the veggies are the first to go, and then comes full-blown bingeing.

Prior to coming to OA, I thought the only two food groups were Fat and Sugar. I've found in recovery that it works best for me to choose a serving from each of the standard food groups at each meal. Although my spirituality is the most important part of my program, the emotional and physical have to be included as well, and vegetables are my key to it all!

When I don't want to eat my vegetables, something is wrong with my spiritual condition. There is usually a kicking, screaming kid in me who is saying, "I will not accept life on life's terms! I will not eat my vegetables!"

After the vegetables go, the next thing I know I'm missing a meeting (or two) and then adding a snack (or two or three) and then I'm bingeing. I've relapsed on three separate occasions since coming to OA, and each time has been progressively worse. During the last relapse I felt like I could have killed myself. Now I realize that's exactly what I'm doing with each compulsive bite.

I've been abstinent now for several months, and things are looking up already. My veggies are up to fifty percent and climbing. The fog is lifting and visibility is much improved. Thanks to a loving HP, a wonderful sponsor, and my veggies, I'm working an abstinent program.

— *Louisiana USA*

Caring for Myself

I write this as the food is calling to me. I have been in OA for four years and have lost seventy-five pounds. I am so grateful that I stayed long enough to receive the miracle of recovery. In the past four years I have seen many come and go. This program hasn't been easy for me either, but I wanted the serenity and peace I saw radiating from the faces around me.

When I came into this program, I was at rock-bottom. My life was a mess, and my weight had begun to affect my health. Today I realize that this is a three-fold disease – emotional, physical, and spiritual – and I have to take care of all three areas to recover. It isn't enough to be willing; I have to do my part to see recovery happen. My Higher Power will help me, but I have to work the Steps and use the tools. This is how I take care of myself.

I take care of myself emotionally by not getting too angry or lonely and by letting others know how I feel in an honest, caring way. I take care of myself physically by not getting too hungry or tired. I eat well-balanced meals, drink plenty of water and exercise. This takes time, but I realize this is the only way to recovery. Spiritually, I spend time with my Higher Power and read literature that will help me to work my program as though my life depended on it. For it does.

— *Alabama USA*

Wake Up!

I got a wake-up call from my Higher Power last week. An OA workshop I'd planned on attending was cancelled because there were not enough people with the time to arrange it. This upset me; I wanted to see others' success, recovery, and commitment to the program. A friend pointed out that I could use this as an opportunity to look at my own program. So I made a commitment to make an OA call, read and write, and pray and meditate every day. I have done these things for a week, and it has made a difference. But today I got another wake-up call – this one much stronger than the first.

I had planned on not attending my Thursday night meeting. I'd gone Wednesday night, I reasoned, so I could easily miss the next day. Then I got a call from an OA friend who told me he would not be at the meeting; he and another member were going out of town for the day. I felt angry. How could he put other things before his program, things that could be rearranged? I soon sensed there was more than anger going on for me.

> *I may indeed be very busy, but I won't have a life if I don't put my program first.*

I have attended many meetings in the last few months where the regulars were missing. In the last two weeks, I have attended three meetings where there were only four or five people. Our intergroup has tried to put on a workshop, get some PSAs out, start a Twelfth-Step-Within meeting and plan some mini-workshops. The results have all been dismal. There was a general lack of interest, lack of commitment, a complacency among members. I finally hit upon what I was really feeling: fear.

I was afraid we might be losing something here – that I might be losing something: recovery. I had become complacent. When regulars stopped coming to meetings, I missed them, but I didn't call. I continued to sponsor, but when was I home to take a call? I used the blanket of "setting boundaries" to give only a little of my time. I called my sponsor and talked maybe three minutes. I started to resent the service I gave to OA. My excuses for missing meetings became less and less valid: "I really need to work through lunch" or "No one wants to hear me, anyhow." I seemed to take it for granted that things would continue, that there would always be an OA meeting. I realize now that this is not true.

I have a fatal disease, and I must remember that. There may be all kinds of pressures and stresses in my life, and I may indeed be very busy, but I won't have a life if I don't put my program first. I have gained so much physical, emotional, and spiritual recovery in the last seven years; I don't want to risk losing it, but I see that is just what I have been doing.

I am grateful to my Higher Power for this reminder. It hurts to look honestly at my program and to see that I can do better. It is time to stop wondering why others don't do service, become sponsors, come to meetings, stay abstinent. It is time for me to renew my commitment to recovery – to redouble my service, to be a more available sponsor, to go to meetings, to be rigorously honest about my abstinence, to call my sponsor, to call other OAers. I need to put my program first, and I want to make sure OA is here for me. My life depends on it.

As I was writing that last paragraph, I got a call from another member who asked me to help get a struggling compulsive overeater to a meeting. That is my Higher Power affirming my commitment and assuring me that I am living the saying, "Thy will, not mine, be done." Thanks for awakening me from my complacency.

— *Texas USA*

The Ghost of Bingeing Past

On a quiet Christmas Eve in the house of an OA maintainer, everyone had gone to bed for the night. Carole lay awake in her bed, though, contemplating tomorrow's planned gathering of family and friends. She thought of two Christmases past, when she'd been losing weight and couldn't partake of the various treats at the party. But this year would be different; she'd been maintaining since March. "Maybe I could taste just a little bit," she thought as she drifted off to sleep.

Klump! Klump! Klump! Carole awoke and sat up quickly. There at the foot of her bed stood a rather obese woman in a torn flannel gown holding a plate of food. Her hair was a mess, hanging down as she stared at her plate. She slowly looked up at Carole, her face smeared with jelly and crumbs and a tear trickling down her cheek. Carole gasped and thought, "She looks just like I did before I came to OA!"

"Who are you?" Carole asked. "What are you doing here?" The sad-faced lady at the foot of the bed said with a shaky voice, "I am the ghost of Christmas-Bingeing Past. I have come to remind you how it was." As quickly as she'd appeared she was gone.

"What a dream," Carole thought, "I must be on a guilt trip about all the food I'll be serving tomorrow." She went back to sleep but was soon awakened, this time by a voice. A woman stood in front of Carole's mirror; from the woman's reflection, Carole could see the hurt and anger in her eyes. The woman was cursing her dress, which she couldn't zip up. She gave up in frustration.

"I don't understand it," the woman said as she looked into the mirror. "I didn't eat any more than anyone else over the holidays! Why me? Well, I'm not going to that OA meeting now that I don't have any clothes that fit right." Carole asked, "Who are you?" The woman in the tight dress replied, "Well, if you have to know, I'm the ghost of Christmas-Bingeing Present. All I had was a couple of small pieces of fruit cake and some eggnog." With that, she vanished.

> "*I'm the one who quit going to meetings because my size-nine dress wouldn't zip up, and my pride was hurt.*"

At 4:00 a.m., Carole felt like she had just dozed off when she was awakened by the loudest, most uncontrolled sobbing she had ever heard. It was coming from the kitchen. She approached the room cautiously; as she looked in, she was shocked! It was a mess; dirty dishes were stacked on the counter with open food containers everywhere. The cupboards were open, and food was all over the table. A woman weighing over three hundred pounds stood peering into the refrigerator, sobbing loudly. "God, please make me stop," she wailed. "I don't want to die of overeating!"

Carole couldn't stand it. She approached the sobbing woman and said, "Who are you? Haven't you ever heard of Overeaters Anonymous?"

"Who am I? Have I ever heard of OA? I'm the lady who was in OA for three years and maintained my weight loss for ten months," the woman answered. "I'm the one who quit going to meetings because my size-nine dress wouldn't zip up, and my pride was hurt. I'm the ghost of Christmas-Bingeing Future, and I could be you!" Carole ran back to her bed as the ghost disappeared. Mercifully, sleep finally came to her.

Carole awoke in the morning without any doubts of her abstinence. She thanked God for the beautiful day and for her family both at home and in OA. As Christmas day progressed, guests arrived and gifts were exchanged. There were also many treats. Each time Carole was asked to sample something, she just smiled and said, "No, thank you. I'm quite full with what I have inside right now."

— *Canada*

Side Dish

"I was traveling down the freeway one day, feeling quite in control," writes P.W., an OA member from New York, "my blood pressure and weight having come down somewhat. I decided to pull off and buy a snack in a vending machine. But when I put the money into the machine, it wouldn't give me the snack. It got stuck on the edge of the shelf and would not come out, no matter how much I shook and pounded the machine! Once again, Higher Power had done for me what I couldn't do for myself."

Feelings to the Fore

I am grateful to be aware of how cunning and baffling my illness can be. After three years in program, it's sobering to see I still get in trouble when I don't use the tools and return to my old self-pity mode. It's humbling to realize I don't have to have all the answers and cannot do it on my own.

For me God's will has always required facing and expressing my feelings, but I don't enjoy it. I usually hid behind a clown mask because I thought that was the only way somebody could like me. Never mind that I held on to resentments while trying to be liked, of course. It's still very hard for me to be assertive when I think it would upset somebody I care about. This past week I had to acknowledge to myself that I was hurt by a friend because he had cancelled our plans twice. Expressing my feelings to him scared me. What if he thought I was making a great deal out of something insignificant? Oh, God, what if he thought I was in love with him!

I was also avoiding telling my sponsor that I needed more consistency in our morning talks. I could understand that her life had changed since her baby was born, and I felt very selfish, but I needed to let her know that my needs weren't being met. Changing sponsors scared me. I also had to face my problem of how to deal with compliments regarding my weight loss. I like the attention, but it's still something very new to me. I have to admit that I'm scared of change.

While all this was inside my head, I sat back and did nothing. I saw the old self-pity in the decision to keep everything to myself – nobody knows! – nobody calls me! Next thing I knew, I was obsessing with food again. I was overwhelmed by the same insanity that had brought me so much pain before. I don't know what I said, but I do know I asked God for help.

I arrived at my meeting thirty minutes early. To my surprise, there was somebody already there. I went to the bathroom and cried my heart out. I told God how lonely and angry I felt and asked for help to share my feelings with the group. The other early member found me and told me it was okay to cry. I was able to tell the group how bad I felt because I thought I should be over this after my time in program. I shared my confusion and my gratitude that I was there. By the time the meeting was over, I felt my commitment renewed. I don't want to imagine what would have happened had I not attended that meeting. When I arrived home the young people's newsletter was in my mailbox. I saw it as an extra message from my Higher Power assuring me that God is with me and as an opportunity to give back what I had just received.

I spoke with my sponsor this morning and was very honest. We agreed on a new arrangement to get in touch. Whether it's going to work or not is out of my control. I did my part and stated my needs. I leave everything else in God's hands. I'm willing to talk to my friend and let go of the outcome, too. I'm also willing to write about the other things that I still don't understand and ask God for insight. Most of the fears I had this past week were all caused by projecting into the future and by thinking I should be over these feelings by now.

I'm very grateful that you were there to have an OA meeting for me. I'm grateful that you understand and care about me. If it worked for you, I know that if I keep working it, it will also work for me. I intend to give God due credit for creating me, and the best way to do that is by letting the real me come out of my hiding place. I'm doing that one day at a time with your help. Please keep coming back: I need you.

— *Florida USA*

An Incredible Feeling

After three years in Overeaters Anonymous, I really thought I had done the Steps pretty well, especially the first three. I was convinced I was powerless over food; I knew I believed in a Power greater than myself; and I really thought I had come a long way in turning my life over to a God I can trust.

So why have I spent these last three years slipping and sliding with absolutely no long-term abstinence, perfect or imperfect? Why do I still find myself eating my old binge foods in spite of what I know and what I want?

My life is immeasurably better, no doubt. I've been a "normal" size for the past three years. I came out of a relapse last year with a gain of only a few pounds – a miracle for someone who can put on five or ten pounds in a weekend. So why couldn't I put the food down for more than a few weeks at a time? Why was I so obsessed with what, when, how much, and where I was going to eat? I made lists of what I was willing to do on a daily basis, and even though the lists included a willingness to avoid my binge foods, I would decide I could handle just one or make up some other excuse. The amazing thing was that I wasn't eating really "bad" foods, or even foods that had once been the mainstays of my food plan.

Last week something happened, and a new process began. I was talking about Step One with a sponsoree, referring her to the pamphlet, "A Guide to the Twelve Steps for You and Your Sponsor," and I read the line: "If he (or she) clings to the lurking notions that there may be an easier way than OA, or that a little controlled overeating is possible, he (or she) will find continuous abstinence unattainable." That was me: my attitude always came down to, "I'll get away with it."

> *So what would happen if I just shoved the whole food problem at God?*

I spent my next morning's two-hour train ride writing. As I wrote, I got angry and very upset. What was coming out was my long-term belief that food was my great equalizer, my entry into society, the thing that made me like everyone else. It had been my only friend when I was young, since I couldn't relate to most of the people in my junior high school. My best buddy was the girl I snuck out of school with to buy desserts at a local bakery, disobeying my parents and using stolen money.

My writing started slowing down as I realized that I was using food so I didn't have to be different from other people. I could fit in. I could be "normal." My terror and dread of being different, of not being accepted or approved of, was being taken care of by food.

Yet I knew food wasn't my friend. I knew that it wasn't bringing me closer to people but was separating me, making me more isolated and different. I may have thought that it was food that helped me survive a hellishly lonely childhood, but it was destroying me in the process. I don't know how I survived my youth, but at that point in my life, food was poison.

My sponsor listened to my writings and suggested that I was very normal—like countless other compulsive overeaters who pursued this course of thought and action into untold misery. This is the insanity of the disease. He suggested that perhaps there was nothing I could do to get rid of my insane dread except to turn the problem over to God.

My attitude began to shift. I sat at a dinner table faced with platters of desserts and realized that not only did I not want any of these things, but that it had been over three years since I'd had any desire to eat them.

I decided that all I had done was turn all these things over to God, and now I had the implicit, childlike trust that God would take care of them. That was it. So what would happen if I just shoved the whole food problem at God? That night I sat down and wrote a short note to God, turning my food, my compulsion, and my insanity over to God's care.

The next morning I woke up with the strangest feeling. I knew with a certainty that all of my binge foods could be put in front of me, and I would have the power to choose not to eat them. What an incredible feeling. I called as many people as I could to share this overwhelming experience.

All I had done was accept the fact that I am powerless over food. I cannot control it in any sense of the word and to try, with lists or willpower, was futile. I was willing to put the food down and accept the gift of abstinence and all that comes with it.

What came with it was God. A Higher Power. And I believe that Higher Power wants me to be sane. All I have to do is take twelve simple Steps that help me change my attitude about my entire life.

I have had periods of abstinence in the past few years, but never on this level. For the first time, I am reacting normally to food. I turned my life over to God, and God is giving me the power to live without my particular brand of poison. And I believe that the God of my understanding will be there with me every day to give me strength and the power of choice.

— *Connecticut USA*

A Plunge to Insanity

"Our Invitation to You" states, "At the very first meeting we attended, we learned that we were in the clutches of a dangerous illness, and that willpower, emotional health, and self-confidence, which some of us had once possessed, were no defense against it." This has been fairly easy for me to accept, since I came to my first OA meeting only after exhausting the easier solutions and finally admitting that I was not able to overcome my compulsion alone. But I have recently experienced a newer symptom of my illness that has provided new insight into the seriousness of this disease.

I was never a binger. Rather, my efforts to cope with life involved eating and/or drinking continuously during every waking hour. Guilt and self-hatred about my weight gain kept me from eating the quantity of sweets I craved, but the result was that I ate things that I didn't even like in order to feed the constant gnawing deep inside.

Abstinence has given me options. I can now choose how to prioritize my activities and focus on work or personal goals. I can view my progress, accomplishments, and mistakes with the loving eyes of a friend and mentor, not the disapproving eyes of a damning judge. In short, although I sometimes struggle with abstinence, my life is filled with people, places, and things that I couldn't appreciate before this program.

So why have I suddenly realized this now that I am only a few bites away from total disaster? Because, while I have been in OA working, stretching, and growing, my disease has not been idle. Recently, I ate a single piece of something sweet after dinner in a restaurant – one bite of impulsive self-indulgence. Immediately, I felt a jolt of electricity racing through my veins, and my mind was consumed with getting to the store to buy a bag of sweets to eat on the way home. This was not mere speculation; it was cold, deliberate planning. I was literally unable to think of anything else. The friends and family around me were no longer important. I wanted only to be on my way to gorge myself in private. Abstinence was not important: nothing mattered but more sugar to extend the high.

What had happened to my program? What about surrendering my will to a Higher Power? It had gone. I hope never to experience that crazed sensation again. By the grace of my Higher Power, when I got to the car I was able to stop and pray, to give my fear and insanity to the Power that has helped me every step of the way. Again, my HP did for me what I could not do for myself. I did not buy the sweets I was scheming to get, but I did eat another item not on my food plan that evening. It was a less-than-perfect recovery from a plunge into insanity. But I am grateful to be abstinent, one meal at a time, and committed to valuing myself and my program by remembering that the "little slips" are nothing less than life-threatening.

— *North Carolina USA*

CHAPTER TWO

"I returned to my isolating ways..."

These members left OA, only to
discover they couldn't recover alone.

Welcome Home

After two years in program and a sixty-seven-pound weight loss, I awoke one morning believing I was cured. This was the first insane thought before the first compulsive bite.

It took six years of overeating and suffering for me to make it back to OA, although I tried to several times. I'd go to meetings searching for a person or sponsor who would say the right thing and fix me. I thought someone else should be responsible for my recovery—or blamed for the lack of it. I didn't realize I had to be willing.

The geographic cure didn't work. Neither did diets. Self-control was nonexistent. I was powerless over food and completely miserable. I continued to pray for an answer even though I thought HP had given up on me.

Three and a half months ago, I read a notice in the local newspaper. Someone was starting a new OA meeting in our small town. Little did I know that this person would become my sponsor and dear friend. I went to this meeting and came home abstinent!

I'm back home again with my OA family. I've learned a lot in the past six years, including the biggest lesson of all: I can't live without OA. In the last three and a half months I've experienced God-given abstinence, recovery from my disease and an under-standing of the program I didn't get the first time around. And I've made many wonderful friends.

In our world of fast foods and quick fixes, my great hope was always an overnight change, a magic pill, an easier, softer way. I was too impatient to wait and too lazy to work long and hard to make it happen. This, I'm grateful to say, is what I used to be like. One thing is for sure—breaking old habits doesn't come instantly.

Nothing takes longer or requires greater effort than practicing the principles of the program in all my affairs. Nor is there any-thing more satisfying than a life lived fully, free from compulsive overeating. Thanks, HP, I'm glad you waited for me!

— *Texas USA*

Bon Jour, Je M'appelle . . .

During the past year, I found myself moving to France with my husband. I spoke very little French and would be living in a city with no OA. After a brief and "white knuckled" abstinence in the States, I was in relapse with no end in sight.

The year before, I had hit my bottom in the same French city that I would now be living in for nine months. This, of course, added fuel to my fears that recovery was not in the near future for me. I visualized myself eating my way through this next nine months, all the time resenting those French women who managed to eat all they wanted and stay "model thin."

> The unity in OA spreads all across the globe. You just have to look for it.

Had I forgotten that not everyone who has this disease of compulsive eating gets obese? Yes. Had I forgotten that not everyone eats like me and has this disease like me? Yes. However, the biggest thing I forgot was that I was in relapse and that my thinking was, yes indeed, "stinking" – worse than some of the smelliest French cheeses.

But several OA members had my address in France and promised to write. I also arrived in France armed with a carry-on bag full of OA literature as well as loads of time on my hands to read, write, and, most importantly of all, develop a relationship with my Higher Power.

The first few months were stressful and lonely. Often I found myself using food as a tranquilizer and as a "friend" (yeah, some friend). I had one OA friend who wrote to me the first week of my arrival. This made me feel terribly homesick for my meetings, yet I also felt hopeful and loved in a manner only one OAer could feel toward another.

I barely knew this friend in the beginning, but I had a gut feeling that these letters were going to be my meetings for a while. With some apprehension, I answered the first letter. What was I getting myself into? Opening yourself up to a stranger, even if it is a fellow compulsive overeater, can feel risky and scary. But my options were limited, and I knew isolation was not going to help my recovery. Thus, I started a challenging yet caring correspondence that has made a great difference in my foreign country experience.

There were others, too, who let me know I was not alone. I received cards from whole meetings, each member there jotting an encouraging, loving note. Another member wrote to me about her own personal struggles in trying to recover from this cunning and baffling disease. This helped me remember that I am not unique in my struggles and that, even though I'm thousands of miles away, I can provide a service too. Those letters, both coming and going, have been a saving grace for which I am truly grateful.

A turning point in my recovery occurred on the day that I received notice of an unexpected package at the post office. I rushed home to open it, bypassing the new *Lifeline* I had just received that day, and found it was from a fellow OAer who had sent me a whole box full of back issues of *Lifeline*! My regular subscription was a blessing, but now I could read new material at least once a week, if not daily, for a couple of months!

I had been trying out the "act as if" philosophy in regard to my Higher Power, and this seemed like a definite sign that indeed my HP was working right beside me and wanted to let me know that.

Earlier this year, I attended the First International World Service Convention in France. I am very grateful for the European OAers who worked hard to make that weekend a reality. So many people were there who spoke my language – and I don't mean English!

OA in France is relatively young, but they have a strength that was evident to me when I walked in the door. If I'm ever back in France, I now know where my home away from home is, and that feels really good.

I won't forget any time soon what I have gained from my time in France. One, I can work a program without meetings and a sponsor. Two, letter writing is a service that I will continue, for it helped my recovery. And three, the unity in OA spreads all across the globe. You just have to look for it.

— *France*

Miracle in Minneapolis

Not long ago, after ten years in program and three years of serious relapse, I scheduled a business trip to the midwestern United States. I would spend two days in Milwaukee, then fly to Minneapolis for two more days and then endure another lonely weekend in a strange hotel, avoiding the hotel mirrors, watching junk TV, and eating alone in my room.

The week went well. But before each appointment, even though I was certain most would go well, I would stop at a convenience store and buy a bag of sweets to see me through the day. I needed them, I convinced myself; after all, I was nervous. What's more, I had earned them. I was driving a rental car on strange roads and frequently lost. If that wasn't suffering, what was?

I also knew that there was a half-pound or more of similar items waiting for me back at the hotel. With any luck, I thought that by the time I returned to my room, the maintenance staff would have thoughtfully removed the mirrors, and I'd be able to eat undisturbed by any visible evidence of just how obese I'd become.

I checked into the hotel in Minneapolis late Wednesday night and ordered dinner from room service. Within half an hour, I was propped up comfortably in bed, watching TV, and diving into my dessert. My finger paused on the remote control briefly as I flicked past the hotel's video event board; there was some sort of OA activity going on at the hotel.

"Hah!" I thought; I'd seen this before. The last time I tried going to a hotel meeting in a distant city, there was nobody there but me. Why try again? I finished my meal and went to sleep.

The next morning I woke, ordered breakfast from room service, showered, and turned on the TV. There was that OA stuff again! I decided that surely it had to be something local – or at best regional. Big deal, I thought: the last time I'd tried a hotel meeting.... I dressed and left for my appointments.

Toward the end of the day, I was driving back to the hotel feeling pleased with my work but consumed with self-loathing.

Eating junk from my purse didn't help. I turned on the radio, thinking some music would make me feel better.

Suddenly I heard a pastor on the radio imploring listeners to pray for deliverance from whatever held them in bondage. "All right, God," I offered. "I'll try it. Please ... I've asked you before. I've asked for the willingness. I'm driving on a strange highway in a strange car and feeling very silly, but I'll ask you again: please release me from the bondage of food!"

> *I emptied the junk food from my purse into OA's wastebasket.*

As I entered the hotel, I planned my evening my way: I would go to my room, order dinner from room service and perhaps check out OA later. But as I entered through an unfamiliar door, I found myself at the foot of the escalator leading to the OA events just one flight above. I let the loving, invisible hand at my back push me gently upstairs and over to the registration table, where I tearfully registered for what I discovered was OA's 1995 World Service Convention. I wrote a check and emptied the junk food from my purse into OA's wastebasket. Later, before bed, I unwrapped each remaining piece of junk food and flushed them all down the toilet.

The miracles did not end there. On Saturday morning, I wandered aimlessly looking for somewhere to be. Spotting another OAer, I struck up a conversation and followed her into an unmarked room. "Oops!" I thought. Then I discovered that it was the gay and lesbian special-interest meeting. I was stunned. My three-year period of relapse appeared to have begun with the recognition, in therapy, of my bisexuality. I had suppressed all thoughts and actions on that subject and had hurt myself terribly in the process. In that circle, I heard my story told again and again and then told mine. It was okay. I was okay! There was nothing to fear here. I could embrace my deepest fears and begin to heal.

As I left early Sunday morning to return the rented car and catch my flight home, I discovered a baby bird resting in the sunshine on one of the hotel paths. I approached with care, speaking softly, musically. Stooping, I offered her my index finger and invited her to hop on, to join me in welcoming this extraordinary day.

She paused, looked me squarely in the eye, issued a ceremonial poop and flew off. Her motion through the air was that gently comic flight common to baby birds and to some newly abstinent in OA: up and down she went. Would she make it? I wondered. I chose to believe she would.

Settling in the area of low bushes across the parking lot, she did. And I knew that through the grace of my Higher Power and the loving Fellowship of OA, I could make it, too – one day at a time, in this program that has already given me so much.

— *New Hampshire USA*

Yo-Yo No More

The "yo-yo syndrome" is a familiar one to many compulsive overeaters. It's typical of us to lose and gain, lose and gain, and lose and gain again, going up and down the scale like a yo-yo, our emotions pulling the string.

Lately I've begun to recognize how this syndrome operates in other areas of my life, such as relationships. "How close do you want me to be to you?" I would ask, in one way or another. "Exactly how should I behave to keep you liking me? Like this? Or like this?" I've also been a yo-yo when it comes to commitments: to jobs, volunteer work, parenting, and, of course, working the OA program.

I went to my first OA meeting in 1982 and my second a year later. That night I found a sponsor. I made daily phone calls to other members, worked the first three Steps and got abstinent immediately – or so I thought. In fact, like the veteran dieter I was, I had simply grabbed a food plan.

This intense commitment lasted about ninety days, through my Fourth and Fifth Steps – until I accompanied my husband out of town to a business retreat. Suddenly I felt out of place, inferior, and lonely. There went my so-called abstinence. The yo-yo took a plunge.

After another few months in OA, I discovered that I needed another Twelve-Step program, one that I judged, in my wisdom, offered greater recovery than I had found in my town's lone, struggling OA group. I didn't exactly desert OA overnight, but my commitment took a nosedive.

Greener pastures beckoned. Why not treat my overeating as a character defect in this other Twelve-Step program? What's wrong with an easier, softer way if it works?

It didn't work. For the next six years I yo-yoed back and forth between programs. When the pain of overeating got too great — when I hit an unacceptable weight level and food again lost its numbing effect — I returned to OA angry, bewildered, and hopeless.

"Why do I keep overeating?" I asked myself. "Why does neither program work on my food obsession?" I was convinced I was living the Twelve Steps. I was active in service work in the other program. So why couldn't I let go of food? Why, in this one area, couldn't I trust the Higher Power I had found early in my OA experience?

I still don't know why, but when I finally committed to OA with my whole being, when I at last became willing to go to any length within the program, to be an OA member among OA members and to share honestly with other compulsive overeaters, the compulsion to overeat was removed.

Last month I completed a ninety-meetings-in-ninety-days commitment to OA. During that time I became willing to ask a woman with a year's experience in the program to be my sponsor. That was hard, because part of me still feels like a veteran. But when I heard her say, "I didn't come to OA to lose weight, I came to stop my insane thinking regarding food," I grabbed her.

I am in OA to become sane and to stop hurting. While food is still an issue in my life, it is not the issue. My priority most days is trying to be open to my Higher Power's will for me and to serve others — both of which are actions I take for my own benefit.

I still hurt sometimes. I still go to extremes sometimes. I still people-please sometimes. But with the compulsion to overeat removed, I have a lifetime ahead of me to learn healthier ways of relating to myself, other people, and my Higher Power.

The yo-yo swings are growing less erratic, and I'm almost ready to let my Higher Power wind up the yo-yo string for good and tuck me away in a pocket, safe and sound.

— *Florida USA*

I Had It Made

For the umpteenth time I joined my favorite weight-loss club. This time, though, I proved to be a success – I got to goal weight, went on the maintenance plan, and attained the cherished Lifetime Member distinction. Then I was encouraged to work for the organization: first as receptionist and later in the ego-inflating position of lecturer. I loved the attention, the power, the inside scoop on diet and nutrition, and I really wanted to help "those people" lose weight.

I had it made. I would be thin for life! But wait, a strange thing started to happen to me. I gained weight – just a pound at my first monthly weigh-in, then two pounds, and finally four. I was above my goal and was ordered to get it off. I had the humiliating experience of being weighed weekly by the receptionist on duty.

I'd heard about OA from a friend and thought it might be the "magic" I needed to lose the weight. I didn't dare tell my employer that I could not diet anymore, so I went to one OA meeting per week. I talked only about my stress of being "over goal," and never mentioned that I binged for two days following my weight-loss class and then starved for two days, even occasionally purging with laxatives.

I couldn't lose the four pounds; I couldn't bear the guilt of what I was doing, yet I couldn't stop doing it. I didn't want to give up my position as lecturer. Finally some OA members helped me see the light, and I resigned. The pressure was off. I had it made once more! I would come to OA once a week, and life would be grand. I didn't understand the program, I didn't work the Steps or use the tools, and that December I left OA.

In six months I gained fifty pounds. Humiliated, I was isolating so I wouldn't see any of my fellow members – from OA or the weight-loss group. I was at the lowest point of my life; I wanted help but could not ask. In pain, I finally reached out to an OA speaker I'd heard at a meeting the previous year. I thank God that she convinced me to go to the meeting that same morning. I finally felt I belonged there, and I desperately wanted OA.

I felt relief and peace at that first meeting. I got abstinent by attending four or five meetings per week, even traveling great distances to reach OA. I listened, read, shared, telephoned, gave service, and got a sponsor who had what I wanted. I still do these things and the promises are coming true for me. Today I am free of the obsessions with food, weight, scale, and dress size. I now accept myself as I am.

I'll keep coming back; for today I truly have it made!

— *Maryland USA*

I'm Back

I have thirty-seven days of abstinence today by the grace of God and the Fellowship of Overeaters Anonymous. It's not my first time around; hopefully I'm back for good – one day, one meal at a time.

I commit myself today to an abstinent food plan. I read a story or two from the *Lifeline Sampler*, I talk to my sponsor, I go to a meeting (at least four or five a week), and I ask God to help me.

I had an opportunity for recovery in 1978 when I attended one meeting in California. Unfortunately, a woman passed the "gray sheet" across the table without even a word of encouragement. I took one look and absolutely knew I could not eat that way, and I didn't come back until 1986 in Hawaii. The "gray sheet" was gone, and I found the acceptance, understanding, and compassion for which I'd been longing. I stayed around several months, bought all the books, found a food plan that worked, went to meetings and "figured it all out." I stopped going to meetings because a man was coming on to me. I didn't know enough to put principles before personalities, so I lost another chance at recovery. I stayed abstinent a few weeks, and then it slipped away.

In 1990 I made my way back again. I put down the alcohol and the pot and got abstinent immediately. I worked a strong program, lost 130 pounds, became a service junkie, sponsored many, and became well-known. I was given eighteen months of beautiful abstinence by God. It was a treasure, a gift, and a blessing, and I threw it away when I heard that someone was gossiping about me because I wasn't yet at a "goal weight." I was badly hurt, but instead of dealing with it I ate and gained almost one hundred pounds.

But I've been back for thirty-seven days. I was compelled to write my story for others who have lost faith, given up, and let the carelessness of others take the beauty of the program from their lives.

I pray to God to help me love myself enough to stay in meetings no matter what I feel about anyone else. I pray to find those who have the capacity to love me back and who love themselves. I pray that I may even love those who hate me. I pray to turn resentment into forgiveness and serenity. I have a long way to go, but I have today. No one can take today away from me.

— *Hawaii USA*

A Balanced Commitment

A recent issue of *Lifeline* asked members to share a personal experience about a time in their lives when an overcommitment to service was used as a means of avoiding feelings or some other unpleasantness. Lots of feelings surfaced when I considered this idea.

Before OA, isolation was the main symptom of my disease. I sat inside my house with the curtains drawn and the telephone turned off. I rarely went out,

We're not unlovable because we have this disease; love is the very thing we need in order to recover.

and social involvement outside of my family was nonexistent.

My life had been so destroyed by the disease of compulsive overeating that when I came into OA, the program became my life. I sponsored, set up meetings, organized events. I even became involved in several other Twelve-Step programs. Twelve-Step literature replaced the mountain of cookbooks on my shelves. Service replaced the obsession with self-improvement.

Overcommitment to service was an escape from having to be alone with myself. The more time I spent on the phone with fellow members, reading literature, and running to meetings, the less time I spent on the things that brought me into the program in the first place.

This method worked really well for a while. I lost one hundred pounds, got all kinds of attention and affirmation from others, and became "proud" of myself. That's where the danger crept in. I might have been a normal weight physically, but my ego had become vastly overweight.

My service involvement was so all-consuming that I neglected my family and started having problems at home. My inflated ego brought me negative attention and caused me to take negative actions in my dealings with others. When that happened I began gaining weight. I gave up all service work and eventually quit going to meetings altogether. After three and a half years in OA, my only connection with the program was my *Lifeline* subscription.

Returning to my old isolating ways, I've regained fifty pounds. There's only one meeting a week where I live now, and my ego gets in the way of my going to it. Since we moved here six months ago, I've attended it once. I've used lots of excuses for not going: "It's at an inconvenient time; it's hard to get transportation." But I keep telling myself the real reason I don't want to get involved in OA again is because it might take too much time away from my family.

After writing this I see that these are not valid excuses. One meeting a week is so much fewer than the number of meetings I attended before I moved here. When I think about it, it seems my

Higher Power is doing for me what I couldn't do for myself. When I lived in a place that offered meetings every day, several times a day, I overdid it. Now that wouldn't be possible.

So what is keeping me away now? It's not really a fear of over-committing to service again. I'm just avoiding people. I'm ashamed of the actions I've taken and afraid of reviving my self-centered craving for the attention of others.

There was a time when I would tell newcomers that they need not feel guilty for actions their disease caused them to take — that guilt serves no purpose and only helps keep us sick. I'd tell them, "We're not unlovable because we have this disease; love is the very thing we need in order to recover." I need to take my own advice.

The pamphlet, "If God Spoke to OA," says that only a fellow compulsive overeater can know the pain we've felt. This is the power of the program: true understanding. I, too, need the love and understanding of my fellow compulsive overeaters. I'm coming back.

— *Singapore*

CHAPTER THREE

"My love and prayers surround you..."

How can abstinent OAers
help still-struggling members?

Dear OA Sister:

A strong sense of sadness and powerlessness settled into my heart after receiving your phone call explaining that you were again in the grips of your eating disorder – and that compulsive overeating was robbing you of the power you need to live happily.

You've been trying for nearly fourteen years to grasp onto recovery from this eating disorder. Because you are a woman of exceptional talent, brains, and personality, I'm convinced that recovery is incredibly difficult for you. I wish I could give it to you as a fine gift – something you could always keep and cherish. You know I would, sweet sister, if I could.

Over the past twelve years, I've clung desperately to my recovery program, for reasons I know you can understand. I've endured a lot of criticism from people inside and outside OA. "Rigid." "Too strict." These are false labels I've had to avoid. I've been able to maintain a slender weight by sticking with my food plan of three balanced meals per day, while avoiding second helpings, snacks and binge foods, which for me include sugar. Most important, by using the tools and working the Steps, I get to live free of the food obsession and of compulsive binge eating.

> *I've found that every difficulty can be overcome, every dream can become a reality... if I keep my recovery first.*

Living a day at a time for twelve years has been an exercise in faith and discipline. Going from single to married, traveling throughout the country, losing my Dad to cancer, moving several times, and finding my way in the working world: these have proved to be my biggest challenges to date. I've found that every difficulty can be overcome, every dream can become a reality... if I keep my recovery first.

I've shared everything I know about recovery with you. The basics never change: establish a food plan, commit to it without reservation, use the tools, work the Steps. And never take that first bite, no matter what.

As I hope you can see through the example of my life, a fresh world opens up on this foundation. Heartfelt dreams are worked toward and reached. A connection to God can be established, a connection that grows profoundly stronger. Physical comfort and well-being ensue. Every day becomes an adventure that fascinates the imagination. It is my experience that this is clearly the truth.

My love and prayers surround you. Please take care, and let's talk soon. Remember: keep your recovery first.

— *Your OA Friend*

A Sad Farewell

My very dear friend died today. Compulsive eating is a killer; it claimed her. She fought a gallant fight, but the drive for excess food won. Oh, Lord, she was so afraid. Let her be with you, light and free of the burden of her body. Let her soar freely with the angels. No more pain, no more fears. Let her be light as a feather. Free of the entrapment of her large body, let her dance.

I don't know to whom I'm writing this. It's a prayer, it's a letting go, it's a warning. Compulsive eating kills; please stop it now!

I met her on a Wednesday morning in 1977, the day I attended my very first OA meeting. She frightened me. Her eyes seemed to say, "Don't get too close." I learned later that was her fear.

I listened to her as I kept coming back to meetings. I listened to her recovery. She chaired meetings, she led, she called me to ask how I was doing. I heard her talk about the Steps, the tools, the "Big Book." I watched her lose weight as she worked a hard program. I asked her to sponsor me, and I was so excited when she said yes. I wanted what she had. She did service at intergroup and began a meeting for teenagers when she saw the need. She edited our newsletter and traveled wherever she was asked.

I watched as she lost 650 pounds. One meeting was held above a fire station where some theater seats had been stored. After the meeting she would try to sit in them. What excitement and joy she experienced the night she found she could fit into one again. She could go to the movies for the first time in years. She found so much joy in life. She arranged OA parties; she loved to dress in costume and play practical jokes.

Somehow the food began to creep back in. She attended fewer meetings and gave less service. Suddenly she was back in the grip of compulsive eating. She tried to come back. She began a relapse and recovery meeting at her home in 1983. I needed it, too, by then. It took hold for me, but it eluded her. I tried to encourage her. I wanted it so badly for her. She had given me so much. I couldn't do it for her; I could only pray.

> *I couldn't do it for her; I could only pray.*

By last year she was in the full horrors of her disease and had eaten her way up to nearly one thousand pounds. She went to the hospital four days ago, but they sent her home. She went again yesterday, but they did nothing for her and sent her home. Today she was hospitalized with pneumonia; she needed a tracheotomy to help her breathe. She ate anyway, and today she died.

Now it will take a special coffin and two cemetery plots for her. Take heed all who believe that one extra bite won't hurt you. It can kill you. It did my friend. I know we won't all eat our way to one thousand pounds, but we're taking years from our lives, risking diabetes, heart failure, and much else. I ache with missing her. I ache for all she could have been. She was only forty-two.

What is your abstinence today? How many meetings have you been to lately? How are you working the Steps? Please don't let me lose you, too!

Goodbye my precious, precious friend. God (my Higher Power) will take you and love you as He always has, and He will watch you dance. He will watch you soar, and I will never, never forget you.

— *Ohio USA*

What's Happening to Our Meetings?

I have recently been away from meetings due to an illness in my family. I've come back to find meetings changed, and I want to let others know how things have changed while I was away.

I do not hear enough about our disease as an addiction and the toll it takes on the body. We need to hear about the seriousness of the isolation, the immobility, and the attitude of just not caring to work on the physical problem.

I hear too much about forgiving one's self after a binge. Early in OA, I learned to strive for clean abstinence; I learned to clean up my food thoughts; I learned to get honest with myself and write, share, or call in before picking up the food. A practice of overeating and then forgiving one's self can become a cop-out; when we depend on the cop-out, it can turn into real denial.

If I had listened to this idea, I would neither have been abstinent for the last three months nor have lost nineteen pounds. I have been attending meetings for thirteen years, and I'm working to change this concept by encouraging others to practice the rigorous honesty that I was taught.

When I see newcomers in my group, I wonder just what they think when they hear this attitude of forgiveness. Looking back on my own first years, I heard, "the more you resist [the food] the sooner you will heal [from this disease]." I was also told, "flour and sugar break me out all over," and this proved true in my case. If I were a newcomer now, I would surely be all mixed up.

I feel our meetings should encourage sharing on "how I worked the tools and Twelve Steps" and "how HP helped me get through this week." In this way, we will pass on to others our blessings and miracles.

— *Pennsylvania USA*

Service Is the Key

I recently learned that a former OA member died of this disease. I feel sad and wonder why I couldn't help her. This is the second OA member in less than two years that I have known to die after dropping out of the Fellowship. Replaying these relationships in my head doesn't give me any answers. I've been unable to Twelfth-Step anyone in my family either. It breaks my heart to sit by and watch people slowly die of this disease.

I find I can't live in their denial along with them. They may get the impression that I think I'm above them because I don't call, but it's difficult to not talk program to someone who has dropped out, and act as if everything is okay. I was in denial about my disease for so long that I can't continue to enable someone else. So I pray that God will lead me to an answer for still-suffering compulsive overeaters.

I continue to give service because service saves lives. I heard that a lot when I first came into the program, but not anymore. In fact, I've heard a funny rumor that people provide service because of their egos. I find that peculiar. My ego would probably like to think I give service to feed it. But the truth is, I need to be of service to stay alive. The "Big Book" tells me to get out of myself, that I can't keep my recovery unless I give it away. The promises tell me that the Twelve Steps will give me a sane, happy, USEFUL life. Service is the key for me.

I've also learned how to say no, so I don't get burned out on OA service. That's the other side of the ego coin. God is in charge of my ego, not me. Yes, I feel a little twinge when I say no when I'm asked to run for a particular office. But I know the source of that twinge is my ego, not God.

— *Anonymous*

In Memory of a Friend

I had a friend who came from Canada to our meetings for over a year. When he came to his first meeting, he was as fat as I had once been. He lost over one hundred pounds – then he stopped coming back. I called him a few times over the last few months. He said he was going to start again, but he never did. He was a genuinely humble, gentle, and loving soul; now he is dead. He died a couple of weeks ago – from our disease.

I wonder if I should have done more to reach out to him – and to all the others who still suffer from our common malady. Do I share some measure of responsibility for his demise? For the deaths of others I've never even met? Did I really do my part to extend the hand and heart of Overeaters Anonymous to those who are as hopeless and desperate as I was when I was alone?

I have to keep joining together with my fellows to reach out to those who still suffer. Their lives may depend on it.

My friend's death has reminded me that this disease does kill people, even the nicest and gentlest among us. And it reminds me that we live or die together. As the "Big Book" says, "no society of men and women ever had a more urgent need for continuous effectiveness and permanent unity." I'll miss him, and I will always be grateful to him for two things that his death illustrates.

The first is that I have to keep coming back; my life depends on it.

The second is that I have to keep joining together with my fellows to reach out to those who still suffer. Their lives may depend on it.

I am as convinced as was Bill W. that we have to keep it simple in order to be effective and responsible. As he wrote in Language of the Heart: "(G)roup responsibility would have to reach much further than the meeting hall doorstep on Tuesday and Thursday nights only. Otherwise the new person approaching our door might miss their chance, might lose their life."

Thank you for being there when I needed you. My hope is that I will always be willing, day after day, to give some of my time, my money, and my talent to this worldwide Fellowship –

to one fellow sufferer at a time, as well as to our outreach organizations.

Personally, I've reached my goal weight and maintained it for over two years. I enjoy a much healthier emotional life and a vital spiritual connection with a Higher Power. I'm getting used to peace and serenity. Thank you for being there along my path to recovery. Keep coming back – for both our sakes.

In memory of my friend, I promise to do my part, one day at a time.

— *Washington USA*

The Price of Abstinence

There are people who come to our meeting every week and complain that they can't get abstinent. But when we offer the solution of the Twelve Steps, they pooh-pooh the idea. They think that holding hands, talking on the phone, and going to meetings should be enough.

It's not enough. I would not have over five years of abstinence today if I hadn't been willing to work the Steps, make commitments, and have a sponsor. My Fourth and Fifth Steps were tedious and time-consuming, and they made me cry. My Ninth Step cost me money, not to mention the humiliation of the social amends. My life was precarious for about a year and a half as I assimilated new behaviors and stifled old ones. And you know what I got for all this discomfort? A comfortable abstinence.

I want to keep this comfortable abstinence, so I'm always providing service to my meeting and sponsoring as many babies as want to work the Steps. I am afraid that if I refused to be of service to this program, I wouldn't need abstinence anymore; I'd have plenty of extra time to fill with binges.

I've lived through plenty in the past five years. I moved, changed jobs, got married, lost two babies, gave birth to a wonderful baby girl, and battled some serious health problems. This is life. I'm a compulsive eater, no different from the other compulsive eaters who come to our meeting and complain and hold hands and talk on the phone and binge. I wish they would listen, work the Steps, provide service, and sponsor. I'm quite sure this program would work for them, just as it works for me and for so many others who have found the willingness.

— *Anonymous*

Abstinence as Sobriety

I spent the first nine months of my OA membership floundering, until one night, when six OA members with at least one year of back-to-back abstinence each travelled 150 miles to share their experience at a mini-marathon weekend. I had never met anyone with over six months of abstinence; I could actually see the glow of their serenity!

These OA visitors stressed that abstinence had to be first and foremost in their lives. Before we left that day, we were all asked to make a list of foods that triggered our binges or caused us to feel guilt or shame. They then asked us if the moment of pleasure was worth these harmful feelings.

The foods on my list are what I consider to be my "alcohol," and if I choose to eat these foods, I've thrown away my abstinence. Before that weekend, I never realized I had the final say about what I put in my mouth. I could say "no"– even to my own diseased mind. Now, with the help of my Higher Power, I can say "no" to these foods without a sense of resentment or loss.

Now, I am free of the food compulsion on most days. I hold on to my serenity by doing these things each day:

• I start my morning with a prayer from the "Big Book," and I thank my Higher Power for my abstinence and for the help I will receive that day, as though I'd already received it. I thank my HP for a moderate and peaceful meal before and after I eat.

• I attend two or three meetings each week and do a nightly Tenth-Step written inventory that I share with a "checklist buddy" once a week. This keeps me rigorously honest.

• I phone my sponsor, who lives 150 miles away, once a week.

Abstinent eating never feels like dieting. When I wander back to my old diet ways, I now recognize it as my disease trying to worm its way back into my life. When this happens, I thank my Higher Power for freedom from my compulsion. I have lost forty pounds in eight months without resentment, anger, disappointment, or hunger.

In our local meetings, where we once had five or ten percent of our membership abstinent, we now have eighty to one-hundred percent of our members with at least thirty days of abstinence. This is a miracle.

Thank you, Higher Power, for bringing those six abstinent OA members with the message we were all so ready to hear.

— *Canada*

The Sponsoree's Gift

Very often I hear struggling newcomers say they don't have a sponsor and can't call anyone because, "I'm afraid I'll bother people." This article is for them and for all who are afraid to reach out. I want them to know how valuable they are to my program.

> *As soon as you make that firm decision to quit OA, go to just one more meeting. It'll be the best meeting you've attended in quite a while.*

I've been a member of OA for four and a half years and have maintained a back-to-back abstinence for almost two years. At meetings I offer myself as a sponsor. Sometimes I think I have enough people to sponsor, but I let God make the decision. Consequently I make and receive a lot of calls – but it was not always this way.

In the beginning my sponsor was the only person I ever called. If she wasn't home and I was in trouble with food, I'd think that I had to stay in my disease because I was afraid to "bother" someone else. My self-esteem was so low that I was afraid I wasn't important enough for someone to talk to. Today I know that I am important, but it took a long time and consistent abstinence for me to realize it.

This past summer God gave me a new challenge. A newcomer who was struggling and needed a lot of unconditional love and attention asked me to sponsor her. God had never brought a sponsoree like this into my life before. What a blessing!

Shortly after I started working with this young woman, twenty-three years my junior, I began to feel that helping her was a way to make amends to my own children for my behavior while in the grip of my disease. I knew that God had put her in my path so that I could take a closer look at how I related to my daughter.

This sponsoree was like a sponge soaking up the program. She'd call to talk food. She'd call to make appointments. She'd call so we could go to meetings together. She'd call and talk for long periods of time, and I felt compelled to stay on the line. I loved her from the beginning with a rare and beautiful feeling that I haven't often experienced.

At the same time, she challenged my thinking. She asked questions that made me look at my program and forced me to grow even when I didn't want to.

And then a serious problem occurred in my marriage. Suddenly there was a huge financial burden and some hard personal decisions to be made.

I felt as if I were drowning. Step One was about the only Step I was willing and able to work consistently. I had no serenity and struggled to maintain my abstinence. The freedom from obsession with food thoughts, a freedom I'd enjoyed for such a long time, had vanished.

I realize today that these thoughts were the result of fear and not hunger. Most of that summer I just barely got myself to the two jobs I was working to keep us afloat. I was exhausted with stress and fear and overwork.

I was overwhelmed by the needs of this newcomer. Since my first relapse thought is: "I am junk!" I tried to push her away with my behavior. I felt I had no recovery to give her, and told her to get another sponsor. She stuck to me like glue anyway. "You're not getting rid of me that easily!" she said. "I want you, and I'm keeping you!" Often she'd challenge me, saying: "I haven't seen you at meetings lately. You can't afford to give up your meetings because you're busy." To my disease, this newcomer was an annoyance. To my recovery, she was a lifeline from my Higher Power!

Never feel like you will be bothering someone when you call or ask them to sponsor you. This is how the program works! Today I am at peace once again, maintaining my abstinence and working all of the Steps. The problems of yesterday are solved. If I hadn't had this persistent sponsoree I might not be abstinent and in recovery today.

I want to thank her, all my sponsorees, and everyone who calls me. It is only in giving my program away, no matter how little of it I think I have to give, that I can keep what I've generously given.

— *Anonymous*

Twelfth Step Within

The only way I can help others in OA is to share my experience, strength and hope, and what has helped me to come out of relapse.

I still hurt and want an easier, softer way after many years in OA. I still don't want to reach out, yet I could die if I try to work my program alone.

I've been greatly helped by people telling me: "I care about you," or "I love you. Is there anything I can do to help?" And my sponsor calling me after I quit calling her to tell me she's concerned and wants to know what she can do for me. This brings to the surface the sadness I'm struggling to resist by staying in my anger and food.

One of the things I was encouraged to do was to go to meetings and talk about relapse and my weight gain. Giving my food plan to my sponsor, even when I have slips or binges, has been a vital key to unlock me from relapse. I never stop going to meetings. They take the power out of my fear and the food.

I'm convinced that working with an active Twelfth-Step-Within committee has brought me out of relapse and into a sane way of life. I tell myself when preparing a sharathon or workshop that if one person shows up, we will have a meeting. Doing the footwork and taking the first three Steps always brings me closer to my Higher Power. It's what the program's all about.

When sponsoring a person in relapse I set up a time for us to get together, a commitment. I give the person what I want myself when I'm in relapse – a listening ear without judgment.

Then I share what I hear and see without shaming them. It's an opportunity for me to take those first three Steps again.

The best gift I can give myself is to keep coming back, no matter what size I am or pain I'm in.

— *Alabama USA*

Hope Renewed

My three years in OA have not been smooth. I've had highs of growth and abstinence, and lows when I've been hospitalized for depression.

I came to the program in desperation. In the addictions of my father and grandparents, I saw the origin of my addiction to food. I found compassion and support in OA, but I discovered a great emptiness within that I didn't know how to fill.

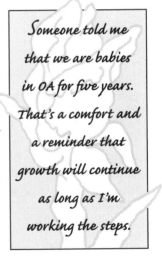

Someone told me that we are babies in OA for five years. That's a comfort and a reminder that growth will continue as long as I'm working the steps.

Two years of abstinence uncovered a depression that had been with me most of my life. I went through months of isolation, self-hate, and thoughts of suicide before I admitted that I needed more professional help and was hospitalized.

After treatment I seemed like a new person. I was happy and had six months of clean abstinence. But then I started slipping and bingeing more and more.

I hung onto the idea that although I wasn't in physical recovery, I was growing spiritually in leaps and bounds. But I continued in relapse. I felt like a hypocrite, surrendering to my HP in the morning and eating whatever I wanted later in the day. My spiritual advisor assured me that I was sincere when I surrendered, but the addiction took over when I binged.

I called an OA friend who had strong abstinence and told her I was desperate to establish my abstinence again. She made up a list of questions for me, one every day for thirty days. I answered them on paper and shared my answers with her.

I became aware that I needed to make amends to myself, go to any length to stay abstinent, and do fun and playful things every day. My hope was renewed.

Someone told me that we are babies in OA for five years. That's a comfort and a reminder that growth will continue as long as I'm working the Steps. Even in my low times I've rarely felt hopeless. I continued to go to meetings, made phone calls, and believed in the program.

— *Pennsylvania USA*

Share the Whole Story

To the newcomer, one day of freedom from compulsive overeating often seems unattainable. Even struggling compulsive overeaters who have been in the program for a while may begin to give up because the handle on abstinence is eluding them. The pain, confusion, disappointment, frustration, and failures become overwhelming and take their toll. Such people feel lost and slide even further down into the pit of despair. Maybe they make one last try. They make their way to a meeting, along with the newcomers, and what do they hear?

Maybe the lead tells a glowing story about abstaining from compulsive overeating for a number of years. She speaks about her substantial weight loss; she says that she is emotionally better off than ever before; she has turned everything over to God, she says, and He takes care of everything.

In the audience is the newcomer who doesn't even know what abstinence is. And the struggling overeater, who just binged on the way to the meeting, can't get a picture of turning over anything to "God." Can they relate to what is being said? Probably not. The distance between them and the lead is so discouragingly far. From where they are, how could they ever reach the level the lead speaks about? Will they come back? Probably not. They leave saying, "Maybe for these people, but never for me."

When we lead or share, are we remembering to tell the whole story? Are we taking ourselves back to our newcomer days or the times of our near-disastrous struggles with our disease? Do we share about how half-measures availed us nothing? Do we share all about the entire journey – the failings as well as the successes? Look at the whole process. We were wounded then; we are healing now. We were discouraged; yet we became encouraged. We had been in the valley, but we became convinced that the height of the mountain was attainable.

The change came sometimes slowly for us, and sometimes quickly, but it did come. There was a lot of pain, but gain too. There was hope. There was help. Even in tears, there were cheers from our fellows. They were always there, and they always will be. There will be new faces among the old, but the spirit will be the same.

Any one of us may give the first message, maybe the only message, that newcomers or suffering overeaters hear. Help them to stay with us. Help them to keep coming back. We need them.

— *Ohio USA*

CHAPTER FOUR

"I choose to continue in this program ..."

A surrender to OA's simple program
renewed these members' abstinence.

I'm a Newcomer – Again!

After almost seven years in OA and several months of solid abstinence, I relapsed recently. I ate over some feelings and, much to my surprise, the food didn't change anything! Feeling a bit foolish, I got back on track by contacting my sponsor and starting all over again. I decided to approach my relapse as if I were a newcomer.

I began by writing down my food plan and reporting it each day to my sponsor. I chose to go to ninety meetings in ninety days. And I began to re-read OA literature with a fresh point of view. One of the pieces I read was the pamphlet, "To The Newcomer" – and it's all there! The words rang true in a new way for me; it was as if I were reading this for the first time.

"We learn that we must honestly admit to our innermost selves that we are compulsive overeaters and are powerless over food." The honesty of Step One reached out and embraced me, calling me to a deeper truthfulness than I had experienced before, renewing my commitment to abstinence.

"The program of recovery is a miracle to those of us who had no hope." The principle of hope from Step Two: there it was in that beginner's pamphlet, waiting for me to "begin" again by reading it anew.

"It is essential in working the OA program that we become willing to accept some Power greater than ourselves." Step Three's principle of faith stirred within me. It's here in this basic pamphlet that I hadn't read in years. I felt stronger as I read on: "We cannot emphasize strongly enough that the spiritual program contained within the Twelve Steps of Overeaters Anonymous works." Of course it does, and I was hearing this good news as if for the first time.

I am grateful today for whoever wrote the pamphlet, "To the Newcomer." It's good to be back; it's good to be home. And it's good to be a grateful recovering compulsive overeater!

— *Maryland USA*

Facing the Challenge

After joining OA I had to find other things to do besides eating. By working the Twelve Steps and using the tools, my obsession for food went away. I would actually forget to eat. This was unbelievable to me.

I had more time to do things, and more energy than I can ever remember. I started walking every day and worked my way up to five miles a day. I was no longer ashamed to be seen in a bathing suit, so the kids and I spent a lot of time at the beach. I played volleyball with a group of singles, and I even started to go dancing. I loved this new life. OA and the Twelve Steps helped me become a real person not obsessed with food.

Someone from my OA group anonymously paid my way to go to my first OA retreat, a gift of love that I consider priceless.

About four months after I joined OA I ended up in the hospital in traction on account of my back. At that time the doctors told me there was something very seriously wrong with me, but they weren't sure what it was. I couldn't work for seven months. Being a single parent of five children, four of them still at home, that hurt financially. The Twelve Steps helped me tremendously when I had to stay in bed for days on end. After seven months and a lot of tests, the doctors still couldn't tell what was wrong.

So I went back to work and started enjoying all these wonderful activities that I had found instead of bingeing. I was amazed at the time and money I had once put into overeating. I was actually saving money now. The new activities didn't cost as much as all the unnecessary food I'd been eating.

A year and a half after joining OA, however, I started getting sick again. I had no energy, I was falling asleep at work, and I started having spells similar to seizures. I started to eat compulsively again. Needless to say I wasn't working the Steps or using the tools. I regained some, but not all, of my lost weight. My doctor sent me to a specialist who thought I had multiple sclerosis, but the tests did not confirm this diagnosis. I had to take five months off work to rest and rebuild my strength. I could no longer play volleyball, swim, take long walks, or dance the way I loved. I was lucky to be able to walk through a grocery store.

Then about ten months later I had to have neck surgery to prevent paralysis. I confronted my doctor about my symptoms before the operation, and he confirmed that I had MS and that I wasn't going to get a lot better.

After the surgery I was involved in a car accident. My whole world caved in on me. I couldn't walk, drive a car, push myself in my wheelchair, do my own laundry, or even leave my apartment without help. And then I was told I'd probably never work again. I'd lost the independence I'd worked so hard to achieve.

I didn't want to live. I wanted the right to die, and I wanted it now. I even figured out the quickest, quietest, cleanest way to end my misery.

Because of the Twelve-Step program, however, I had been writing about my feelings in my inventory, and, of course, I had to give these thoughts away to my sponsor. What a gracious lady. She listened and cried with me more than once. Then I had the courage to tell another OA buddy, and, before I knew it, I was leading my first meeting in over a year, telling my story to my OA group. I shared a part of myself that I couldn't talk about with my doctor or my family. My OA friends cried with me and hugged me. My wonderful sponsor sat right by my side to give me extra strength. Since that meeting I have not eaten compulsively, and I'm definitely alive. The obsession to eat has gone, and I lost the weight I'd regained.

I've again found peace and serenity from compulsive overeating. I don't like being handicapped, but it sure could be worse.

Someone from my OA group anonymously paid my way to go to my first OA retreat, a gift of love that I consider priceless. I'm finding different things in my life to do – writing this article is one of them, since I've never written anything before. I thank God, my sponsor, and my OA group. Because of them, my children still have a mom.

— *Michigan USA*

My Personal Boulder

Well, there I sat. After some time in OA, I found myself discouraged, defeated, and eating compulsively once again. I was tired of my disease and my lax, wishy-washy program. I couldn't seem to grasp the program concepts – the Steps intimidated me, and I was very on-again/off-again about using the tools. It just seemed like too much to cope with, and I despaired of ever getting the hang of working a good solid program. An upcoming OA retreat seemed like a good place to escape to, so I signed up.

At the retreat, the speaker asked us to participate in a five-minute meditation exercise. We were to visualize a favorite place. With us at this place was to sit an elderly person whose identity we were free to determine. Amid this peaceful scene we were to place a large boulder. That was the scenario, and we were asked to meditate silently on this and attach our own feelings and experiences to the scene. I would like to share mine with you, my OA family.

The place I chose as my special spot was beside a beautiful path in the woods, much like the path along which I had taken my morning walk that very day. The scene was quiet and beautiful – trees, birds, and a lovely deep stream with a small waterfall. It was early morning and the sun shone through the trees, highlighting the dew on the grass and leaves.

I placed my imaginary boulder right in the middle of the scene in a pool of deep water, blocking my access to the prettiest part of the woods. I knew instinctively that the boulder represented my disease of compulsive eating. The "elderly being" was God, my Higher Power. He appeared as a loving Father sitting quietly at the side of the woods.

I imagined myself walking into the scene and sitting down on a small rock. I wasn't really comfortable on this rock, but I didn't shift position or do anything else about it. I just sat there. This represented to me my half-hearted commitment toward my OA program and my feeling that I was at a standstill and making little progress in my recovery. The effort to shift positions just seemed too much. I knew the boulder of my disease was blocking my way, and I wanted to get beyond it and move on to the beautiful woods (my life) on the other side.

I waited, with God still beside me, sensing that He loved and accepted me, His compulsive child, just the way I was. But I knew He had so much more for me if I'd only reach out. I spent nearly the whole five-minute meditation just sitting there – me, God, and my personal boulder. I was waiting for Him to lift or push the boulder aside so I could effortlessly stroll through to the other side, but He didn't. At last I came to realize that that's just what I'd been doing in my life; waiting for God to do it all for me without doing the foot-work myself.

> *I knew that, with God's help, that pathway around the boulder is passable and leads to a fuller, richer life.*

As this realization hit me, God arose from His seat and beckoned me to approach the boulder. I did so tentatively, feeling that I was powerless to get around it or move it and afraid of the deep water surrounding it. That's when God pointed down into the water and I saw that there were Twelve Steps around the boulder. I was afraid to step out. I had tried and failed so many times before, but God took my hand, and I knew it was safe to try with Him walking along beside me. I stepped onto Step One and found that it was sure and solid and it held me up. I moved on to Step Two and then Step Three, and each time I faltered or began to lose my balance, there He was right beside me steadying me. I must admit that Step Four was rocky and a little slick. That inventory Step never has been smooth going for me! But again, God steadied and encouraged me, and I was able to negotiate that Step.

Along the way there were various outcroppings of rock on my boulder, places which were very difficult to get around. That's when God handed me tools – the ax handle said "ABSTINENCE," the hammer said "SERVICE," the chisel said "LITERATURE," and so on. I whacked away on that boulder with the tools, and they made it possible to get past the especially rough places. I was dreading Step Nine in particular (that, to me, oh-so-difficult-sounding amends Step!), but I found it wasn't so bad after all.

In time I made it all the way to the twelfth and final Step and the boulder was behind me, not gone, but no longer looming over me, blocking my way to all that was beautiful ahead. I knew that I hadn't walked the Twelve-Step path for the last time, and I would be called on to walk it again and again throughout my life. But I found that I was no longer afraid to step out. I knew that, with God's help, that pathway around the boulder is passable and leads to a fuller, richer life. The meditation ended, and I opened my eyes. I had learned a lot about God, myself, and my program in those five minutes. I felt recommitted and hopeful. And, yes, I found that God was still there beside me holding my hand.

— *Arkansas USA*

Not Just for Teens

When I came to OA on January 18, 1988, I was vomiting eight to ten times most days, weighed under one hundred pounds and had been bulimic for twenty-two years. When I had haltingly discussed my problem with my family doctor, he looked perplexed and said, "Bulimia? But you're not a teenager!" I replied, "I was a teenager twenty-two years ago. It just goes on and on." That is, if one doesn't die first.

At that time my life revolved around food, my body size, and the numbers on the scale. I had to create inventive ways to get rid of my husband and children in order to binge on incredible quantities of food. If compulsive overeaters think they consumed a huge amount of food before OA, I would challenge them to just imagine the possibilities if they were able to binge, vomit, and then start all over again. I think sometimes members who have a great deal of weight to lose think perhaps it is easier for the person who begins the program at or below a healthy weight. As a recovering bulimic, I had to learn to abstain from a colossal amount of food every day. Because my disease didn't show up on my body as excess pounds, there also didn't seem to be any pressing reason to stop this lifestyle, unless you consider that my life was ruled by insanity and that I was literally killing myself.

For years before OA, I knew that what I was doing was insane and self-destructive, but I was powerless to stop. I had tried psychiatrists, and even hypnosis, with no success. When a counselor led me to OA, I had become convinced that I was going to die of what I then felt was my gluttony, but what I later came to know as my disease.

To my amazement I became abstinent at my very first meeting. However, I have realized that my early abstinence was about finding support to control my food. I maintained a weight of around one hundred pounds for ten months and then went into relapse. This was not an honest weight for me, one that my body couldn't maintain without rigid dieting. Over the next few years, I experienced varying periods of abstinence from compulsive eating and vomiting, but still retained control at 110 to 115 pounds. During this time, I worked the Steps to the best of my ability, got a sponsor, did two Fourth and Fifth Steps and, despite slips and periods of relapse, continued my journey in the direction of recovery. At no time did my slips remotely resemble the eating festivals I indulged in before OA, nor did they give me happiness or gratification. Thank you for that, OA!

On April 6, 1992, I made a breakthrough when I reached bottom and had to admit it was time to turn my will and my life – which included my body-size and weight – over to my Higher Power. It was time for me to allow my Higher Power to decide what I should weigh. I also realized that my abstinence had to have "no vomiting" as its basis. I must be responsible for the food that goes in my mouth. Gradually, over the past years, my weight has leveled out at 120 pounds – a healthy size seven, as opposed to an emaciated size three.

The plan of eating that works for me is four meals a day, with the flexibility to eat in-between if my work schedule demands too long a stretch between meals. I travel a long distance to attend one meeting per week, which I cannot miss if I am to retain my serenity and my abstinence. Most important of all is that I have a wonderful sponsor who loves me enough to tell me if a character defect is rearing its ugly head. Her love, kindness, and sanity have gently steered me through the Twelve Steps; she has shown me that the answer to my eating disorder, as well as to all of my life problems, is to be found in the Steps. We have laughed together. We have cried together. And, through it all, we have become dear friends.

The promises of the program are all coming true for me. I have, for the first time in forty-four years, a loving relationship with my family of origin. It is due to OA and the Twelve Steps that I have three happy, well-adjusted teenagers of my own. My dear husband, who has stuck with me through the hell of bulimia, is finally able to relax and live for his own needs, instead of perpetually trying to save a wife bent on self-destruction.

Just for today I am abstinent from compulsive overeating and vomiting; I am growing emotionally with the help of my sponsor; I have a belief in and a relationship with my Higher Power, whom I choose to call God. I am so grateful to the Fellowship of OA for giving me a life.

— *Canada*

That First Step

Powerlessness. When I read this word in Step One, I thought it meant that I was going to be powerless over food and have an unmanageable life for the rest of my days. At first OA meant finding people with whom I could share my powerlessness and unmanageability.

My first year in OA, I lost weight by dieting and used powerlessness as a crutch. When I overate, underate, manipulated, compulsively spent, or gained or lost weight, the "powerlessness" was the perfect crutch to justify my insane behavior.

Each meeting became a powerlessness party for me. I felt euphoric finding people to share my insanity and no one telling me to stop it!

After a year of depending on this crutch, I relapsed and gained back thirty pounds. I was devastated.

Someone gave me a book and told me to read the words of Step One again "word for word." I did. I began to realize that the admission of powerlessness was only the beginning of Step One – a point from which to move forward.

> Today I see that I used my "powerlessness" crutch to avoid the real work.

As I read further, I began to see an alternative to the unreality that had characterized my life of compulsive eating and bingeing. I had a glimpse of a new reality that could be mine.

Today I see that I used my "powerlessness" crutch to avoid the real work – making changes, feeling feelings, doing the footwork, writing the inventory, seeking my Higher Power, and taking responsibility.

My life has changed. I have written my inventory. I go to meetings and share my mistakes as honestly as I can. I have done the footwork, made the amends, sought a conscious contact with my Higher Power, and gotten the resulting rewards.

I know the Twelve Steps are designed to get me well, not keep me sick. My sanity was restored and my compulsion removed, together with my excess weight, as a result of living these twelve suggested Steps.

My Higher Power has given me the ability to react sanely around food today. I don't want to be powerless over some item in my fridge or be afraid of a dessert. I want to have the power to say, "No, I choose not to eat that." And I believe that's what my Higher Power wants for me, too. Now I see the First Step as a point of reference from which I move on, not a position I take for the rest of my life.

— *Scotland*

Wake-Up Call

At my home meeting a focus for discussion has sometimes been "the wake-up call – the event or circumstance that led us to seek out the program or surrender to it." For me, the wake-up call was my doctor telling me that, as a 260-pound diabetic, I could be dead in ten years. When I heard this, I laughed. I reminded the doctor that my parents were in their nineties, enjoying quality lives. The doctor said very simply: "Where do you want to be in ten years? Able to walk down the street – or in a wheelchair or a nursing home?"

I was approaching "the big six-oh," and I was depressed. I'd gained back 85 of the 125 pounds I'd lost in OA since joining in 1976. My job was strangling me, my relationship was like open warfare, and I was a classic couch potato.

I was active in OA. My main hobby was service at the intergroup level. But people didn't do things my way, so I brooded, feeling like a dinosaur. I had no sponsor, and nobody wanted anything I had.

My lack of abstinence was all-encompassing. People in program would tell me that, with all I'd done for others, all I had to do was ask for help. But I had too much ego to simply admit I was whipped.

Finally, I asked God for direction. The light bulb went on, and the simple answer came: "Admit you're in relapse and start anew." So I did.

I asked another man, who had many things that I wanted, to be my sponsor. I'd call him every morning and we'd talk – about food, spirituality, baseball, work problems, money problems, family problems, or health problems. He'd suggest meditations and other things for me to read.

I started getting up and sharing at meetings. I also went to chip meetings and took chips. I committed my food and ate what I'd committed. I carried my lunch to work. I began praying again and stopped being an expert.

A year passed, and I'd given back forty-five pounds. People

started asking me to sponsor them and to lead meetings. As I write this, I've been abstinent for sixteen months, and I'm close to one hundred pounds below my top weight, seventy pounds of which were lost since my doctor's warning.

> *Finally, I asked God for direction. The simple answer came: "Admit you're in relapse and start anew." So I did.*

My job is tolerable, my relationship is far more loving, and I'm spending less time on the couch. I've made amends to my elderly parents, and I'm still "cleaning house." The desire to eat has been lessened, and I rarely feel deprived or threatened by any kind of food.

I'm grateful to God for this second chance. I realize that I'd enjoyed physical recovery fifteen years ago but let it slip away.

I had to admit that I was in relapse. Once I surrendered, I repeated the actions that led to my initial recovery and stopped taking the actions that were killing me. I'm certainly glad I was home when that wake-up call came.

— *California USA*

No Separation

I began my OA recovery five and a half years ago with the realization that there was not enough chocolate or cigarettes in the world to make me feel better. I was seeking "a better relationship with food" and a spiritual community, so my therapist recommended OA.

I'd never had a sense of belonging in the world, but my compulsive eating really escalated at age nineteen when I moved out of my parents' house and became sexually active. I finally entered OA when I was thirty-five years old, after a very intense sixteen-year history of heavy, late night sugar binges, followed the next morning by running for miles and miles to purge all those calories. My weight never fluctuated more than twenty pounds, but I was gripped by the insanity of the obsession: how to binge without being seen, how to rotate stores so the clerks wouldn't recognize me, where to hide the wrappers – a miserable existence, indeed.

In these past five years, I have worked Steps One through Nine, and I now continue working Steps Ten, Eleven, and Twelve every day of my life. These are the Steps where I get to practice the principles contained in all nine of the previous Steps, as well as I can, here and now.

For example, memories of childhood sexual abuse surfaced during my Fourth-Step inventory. Through the grace of my Higher Power, I found the support I needed in the OA Fellowship to endure those memories. In the years since then, I have seen repeatedly how I can use the tools and work the Steps in relation to anything that comes up in my life. When I have the problems, the Twelve Steps are my answers.

Today Step Ten is about regular writing, regular inventories, regular contact with a sponsor and with other OA members. Step Ten is about commitment, honesty, willingness, surrender, assuming responsibility for my actions, and making verbal and living amends. I cannot remain in recovery unless I am willing to change my attitudes and my ways of relating to others. Step Ten is about showing up and doing the footwork in my life. It's about accepting all parts of myself and changing what I can.

> I suddenly saw the delusion of forty years of fear, isolation, shame, self-will, and pride, and I saw their poverty in contrast to this divine reality.

Using the Twelve Steps and the tools, and then leaving the results to a Higher Power works. It sounds so trite, but it's so simple and so true. I have learned this truth for myself through struggling with maintaining my abstinence for the past three years. One recent night, I shared with another member that "the food is still working for me. I'm just not desperate enough."

I hung up the phone and binged. When I woke up the next

morning, I knew: I was desperate. I had reached a deep, deep bottom where the food no longer worked for me. As I drove out of town for the day with a friend, I shared all my secrets and recent fears. I prayed for the willingness to let go of everything that keeps me trapped in my pain and shame and self-abusive behaviors – not just the food obsession. It was more than that. I prayed for the willingness to walk, empty-handed, into the domain of God's truth.

And so the action of Step Ten paves the way for the receptivity of Step Eleven. In my experience, there really is no separation between these last three Steps. There's no way to separate the continuing self-examination of Step Ten from the spirituality of Step Eleven or the service of Step Twelve. And I realize, too, that I've never really been separate from God, after all; I've only believed myself to be alone. Step Ten – doing the daily footwork – is a spiritual practice for me.

That evening after my surrender, I saw some rapid cloud movement in the sky that I'd never seen before. I thought maybe I was just fooling myself, but I know now that God was showing me reality. I suddenly saw the delusion of forty years of fear, isolation, shame, self-will, and pride, and I saw their poverty in contrast to this divine reality.

When my sponsor asked me what I needed to maintain my abstinence, I answered that I needed more contact with her, more contact with OA folks, and more service. So I've made afternoon phone calls every day for three weeks now, committing to myself that I will have no food after dinner and that if I decide to eat something, I will call someone before doing so.

OA has shown me, directly, that I never, never have to be alone. Step Ten has shown me that it is my daily choice whether to continue in this program toward recovery. Today I choose sanity, serenity, and peace.

— *Anonymous*

"I Lost All Hope . . ."

Winston Churchill said, "Never, never, never quit." Great leaders work toward excellence, not perfection. This means they make mistakes; they fall down and get back up to try something new until they succeed.

I will soon celebrate three years of recovery in Overeaters Anonymous. My story tells of a one hundred-pound weight loss with eighteen months of squeaky clean abstinence. However, when I got to Step Nine the third time around, I was unwilling to make amends to the one person whom I'd abused the most: me.

My period of relapse was brief. It lasted through four months of denial and overeating. The one thing I didn't give up on was my meeting attendance. I went at least two or three times per week, performing service at both the group and intergroup levels. I just had forgotten some of the basic principles of the program, like hope, humility and honesty. Mostly, it was my own mind that got me into trouble.

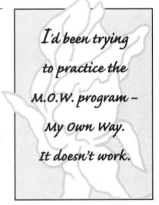

I'd been trying to practice the M.O.W. program — My Own Way. It doesn't work.

I thought I knew enough to get by. I was going to show some people that I really knew what I was doing. But what happened was I lost all hope and began to think I didn't need Overeaters Anonymous after all.

After a while, some of the so-called open sharing in meetings became negative pitches that I didn't want to hear. I stopped sharing my recovery and started to isolate in meetings. I was there in body, but absent emotionally.

It didn't take long for my dishonesty to show up as a dramatic weight gain of over forty pounds. At first, I rationalized the weight gain and felt that if others said they were abstinent, so would I. But I encountered reality when someone asked me if I was pregnant. She was embarrassed when I remarked that I was not pregnant, just practicing my disease. I was desperate. I'd been so out of control with the size of my portions, as well as with the quality of my food, that I needed a very clear, strong message from my Higher Power. I'd been trying to practice the M.O.W. program – My Own Way. It doesn't work.

Somehow, God blessed me with some clarity. I knew that if I did not get help, I would be back up to my all-time high of 240 pounds. I looked around the room at our big meeting; there was someone there with nine years of abstinence who seemed always to speak his truth. He shared with me how I could have "perfect" abstinence. Right there, I committed to a newly defined plan of eating with boundaries I could live within no matter what.

Eventually, this same person agreed to guide me through the Steps to a spiritual awakening. This incredible path has literally changed my life, and I pass on this legacy to all who are willing to be sponsored in this powerful program.

In the past ten weeks, I have completed the Twelve Steps in seven weeks and finished all thirteen of my amends. Some of my amends are an on going attempt to incorporate spiritual principles in my life. This is the first time I've ever worked all Twelve Steps with one sponsor, and it is the first time that I held nothing back. I was able to get to the exact cause of my wrong-doings and own up to my own responsibility in my problems. It's very freeing to start with a clean slate, but I'm also very raw and vulnerable. It's all so new to me: I'm clearly present and conscious now.

The most difficult part of the relapse was admitting it to my group. Since I do believe there are no mistakes, I know there was a reason why I relapsed. But it still hurts to know that no matter how hard I tried, I still lapsed into the pain, alone. There were few people who talked to me at meetings; I think they thought I was contagious. I'm eternally grateful that no matter how manipulative I became, God did not give up on me.

One of my greatest lessons from this relapse has been humility. The core of this principle is to always remain teachable. I sometimes get amnesia, though, which is why I still go to meetings.

Relapse is a part of my story, but it doesn't have to be a part of yours.

When the pain is great enough, I'm motivated to do something. Believing and acting are not the same. If I really want something, I'll take action. I'll just do it. So learn from my experience: Do it now, while you have the chance, before it's too late.

— *California USA*

Enthusiasm Regained

During my first eight years in OA, I was often asked how I kept my enthusiasm for working my program. To be honest I never really knew how to answer because the excitement of recovery never diminished for me. I was always grateful that I no longer weighed three hundred pounds and was not obsessed with food. Each day I humbly thanked God for my new existence and offered myself for further service and growth.

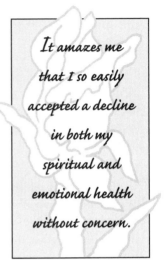

It amazes me that I so easily accepted a decline in both my spiritual and emotional health without concern.

I don't know when things started subtly changing inside me. Perhaps it started with making judgments of others. Self-righteousness feels so good that I might have let it slip by on my daily inventory. Perhaps it started by hiding a bad motive under a good one in order to rationalize my criticism.

Looking back I realize that my spiritual life was affected first. I overloaded myself with school, work, and family, and no longer had time for OA service, prayer, or reading program literature.

This decline in my spiritual life soon engulfed me emotionally. My teenage son's problems scared me deeply, and this tremendous fear was accompanied by self-pity and resentment. In retrospect it amazes me that I so easily ignored and accepted a decline in both my spiritual and emotional health without questioning and without concern.

Food was not far behind me now. I started snacking at movies again, something I hadn't done in a long time – and I'd added a nighttime snack. I often felt very full and, after each weekend, wore my "fat clothes" for a couple of days. If I wasn't in full relapse, I was very close.

Had I forgotten that this disease is a fatal progression? How could I have been so insane? Most distressingly, only a part of me cared. The other part just felt tired and apathetic.

I know that God sent me some strong messages during that time, but today I can't tell you exactly what happened or when. I only know that God stayed with me during this hard time, and I didn't stop praying even though it felt at times like I was merely reciting words. I began attending more meetings, and my group started a new Step study from OA's new Twelve-Step book. I became acquainted with several newcomers who brought fresh insight into our meetings, and I read a *Lifeline* article from an old-timer in the program that really touched my heart.

Once again I felt the joy of recovery. My abstinence was good, my emotions were stable, and my conscious contact with God was once more my primary concern. I am certain that once again I am alive by God's grace.

— *Texas USA*

Sixty-Two and Counting

When Overeaters Anonymous and I discovered each other, it was love at first sight.

Within a few weeks I was committed to working the Steps and embracing and being embraced by my kindred spirits in OA. At long last I was home.

At the same time I was beginning to deal with the lifelong damage of childhood sexual abuse. Besides attending OA meetings and reading OA literature, I was waist-deep in therapy, survivors' groups, flashbacks, and more pain than I knew existed. So I was understandably proud when my sixty-day chip took its place next to my thirty-day chip on my key chain.

And then the unexpected happened: I became overwhelmed.

Deeper memories surfaced, the pain multiplied, and I lost my precious abstinence along with my faith in my Higher Power.

Another thirty days passed as I struggled with the anger, guilt, pain, and sense of having lost something irreplaceable. No matter how hard I tried, I couldn't get my abstinence back.

Although I felt awkward and ashamed, the continued love and acceptance of my sponsor and other friends in OA brought me back to meetings again and again. It wasn't the same as when I was abstinent, but I knew it was where I needed to be.

And then it happened. I regained my abstinence. First for one day, then two. I looked once more at those first precious chips and wondered if I should take them off my key chain. The thought of losing them and starting from scratch was very depressing.

Suddenly I knew I hadn't lost them at all. I wasn't starting from scratch. Even though I had lost my abstinence, I still had recovery. Throughout those thirty dark days I never left OA. I still carried it in my heart and mind and soul.

So once again I'm counting the days. I had sixty days of abstinence before I got off track, so that's where I'm picking it up again. Sixty-one, sixty-two – and still counting. It's so good to be back home.

— *Indiana USA*

Back to Basics

As I understand it, the purpose of abstinence is to take us to the point where we'll no longer have to try to be abstinent; rather, it will happen automatically.

In the early 1980s, OA's focus seemed to be on physical recovery. Far more often we heard slogans that implied that abstinence may hurt at first: "No pain, no gain." "This, too, shall pass." "One day at a time." "Easy does it."

People came into OA to lose weight, and OA gave them a definite food plan. I'm continually grateful that I found OA during this period. I desperately needed discipline in my life. Nothing was left to chance. Everything was spelled out for me: if one did x, y would happen.

I did everything exactly as it had been laid out for me. I got a sponsor, abstained, and worked the Steps – all of them, in order. The first thing I noticed – because it was all I'd really been looking for – was that my clothes were becoming looser. Soon I realized that I had more energy and enthusiasm for life. My self-esteem began to soar and for the first time in my life I felt I had rights, including the right to just be alive.

> I'm recapturing my zest for the program by making it a challenge again.

After several years of riding the crest of this wave, a number of sudden reversals took place in my personal life, and I crashed. The result was a complete deflation of my ego. I see now that this had been necessary in order to establish a firm foundation on which to build my new life, but at the time I didn't want to live. I still had OA, but unfortunately my personal program hadn't progressed far enough, and I lost faith in it.

For a few months I attended Alcoholics Anonymous meetings daily. It might be more accurate to say I absorbed them. I admired the dedication and commitment I saw there and was once again convinced that Twelve-Step programs do work.

One recurring phrase I heard was: "Don't drink, and go to meetings." I thought this was the same as saying, "Don't eat, and go to meetings" to a compulsive eater. I realized it was time to go back to OA.

Having been restored to a degree of sanity and attained enough humility to cover my bruised ego, I attended a newly formed OA meeting. But it wasn't the same program I remembered. The emphasis had shifted almost completely away from physical to spiritual and emotional recovery.

The definition of abstinence as I knew it was equated at this meeting with dieting and vigorously opposed. Abstinence was left open to private interpretation, which in my case became a license to eat.

After a few years I was back to the weight I was when I first started the program. I became nostalgic about those early years in OA when I did what I was told because the one who told me had already done it herself. That had been a time when I'd learned a valuable lesson; that whatever I practiced got easier, whether it was eating or abstaining.

I wonder what we have to offer newcomers seeking physical recovery if we don't define and stress abstinence. Since they can't see our spiritual or emotional recovery, the only proof of our success – or lack of it – is what they see and hear.

We in OA have always said that we have a threefold disease. Obviously our recovery must also be threefold. I believe we must be as specific about abstinence as we are about working the Steps. If we honestly believed compulsive eating is a disease like any other, would we still be so hesitant about treating it?

I'm convinced that the things that don't kill us eventually make us stronger. This was certainly true of my early years in OA. I'm recapturing my zest for the program by making it a challenge again. In the meantime, I'll leave you with this deceptively simple slogan: "Don't eat, and go to meetings."

— *North Carolina USA*

Season of Rebellion

Shortly after I celebrated two years of abstinence, I started to become very rebellious in my program. I didn't want to do it anymore. I didn't want to weigh and measure my food. I didn't want to be on a food plan anymore either. I'm at a normal weight, and I resented that I was still different from other people when it came to food. I didn't want to be a compulsive overeater anymore. I just wanted to be normal and able to eat sensibly without all the boundaries. I hated all the meetings I was attending. Everyone at the meeting was struggling with abstinence, and I felt they had nothing to offer me. I couldn't do any writing and didn't want to even if I could. I couldn't even talk about how I was feeling for a couple of weeks. I was scared and holding it all inside.

When I did start talking about it to my sponsor and other OA friends, I was complaining more than anything else, and I really didn't want to be helped. I just wanted someone to listen to me whine.

I told my sponsor that I couldn't write, and she told me to pray for willingness to write. I hated that answer. It was so cliché. I had gotten to the point where I wasn't even willing to be willing. I recognized that I was in the relapse process.

> *I was two years in program and still whining about my food. I realized that it was time for me to grow up.*

I looked back over my first two and a half years in OA. I released one hundred pounds during my first year in program and have been maintaining that loss. In my first year I learned how to arrest my disease by placing my faith and trust in a Power greater than myself. This allowed me to surrender to a plan of eating and live by a set of rules that I didn't make. In my second year I continued my practice of abstinence and the quest for spiritual growth. Now, in my third year, I found myself in a relapse.

I know that anyone who has an addiction and is recovering from that addiction will have a tendency to relapse. It's just the nature of the beast. And this wasn't the first time that I'd felt myself slipping back into negative attitudes and destructive behaviors. I am constantly aware of signs of relapse; that's the only way to stay in recovery. I listen intently to people who have relapsed. They have all said that the relapse didn't start at the point when they started addictive eating again. Their relapse started when something in their lives didn't feel right, and they didn't know what it was nor how to deal with it. The only way they had ever known to make those uncomfortable feelings go away was to stuff them down. I needed to find out what it was in my life that was making me feel uncomfortable. Clearly, I didn't know, and this unknown was manifesting itself in my defiance and rebelliousness. I was very afraid because, although I've felt myself in the relapse process before, this time was the farthest it had gone. I was in a really negative place.   I had not gone back to the food, but I could feel that it was just a matter of time if I didn't deal with myself soon.

When I realized that I wasn't even willing to be willing, I prayed. I told God that I was scared and that, although I was praying for help, there was still a part of me that didn't want to be helped. I cried and told God that I was in pain. After my prayer I didn't feel any different, but somehow I knew that I had let go of the problem and had turned it over to God. That weekend, I went to an OA retreat. I had felt myself starting to come through the rebelliousness, but I didn't experience complete clarity until I wrote an inventory and gave it away as part of an assignment at the retreat.

My writing revealed something that had been eluding me. There had been a yearning inside me. Something in me wanted to grow, like a plant that has outgrown its pot. The yearning was for a more conscious contact with God, to discover the person God intends me to be. I saw that I needed to seek out opportunities that would bring my will into alignment with God's will.

In my writing I saw that I had passed up several opportunities in the last few months. I denied myself a chance to be in a dance show, something I have always wanted to do. I also passed up auditioning for a play and applying for a different job. All of these things I failed to do because of fear. Fear of commitment. Fear of success. Fear of failure. Fear of rejection. Fear of having to be honest about my past.

Because my feelings can be so elusive, all of this manifested in rebelliousness and wanting to eat. My writing revealed to me that I had been stifling my spirit. My inner voice was telling me to seize life, to go for whatever I wanted and to leave the results up to God. My disease had been keeping me paralyzed in fear.

The writing assignment asked me what I could do to work out my problem. What could I do about my fear of taking risks? I already knew what to do because I had already done it by coming to the program of Overeaters Anonymous. The program teaches me to let go of my fears and to trust God. Holding on to my fears is a form of taking back control of my life and letting self-will run riot. I can change by doing my footwork and leaving the results up to God. Go audition for the play, apply for the job, just try. If I don't try, I'll never know if I like it or hate it. Most of all, I'll never know if it was God's will for me or not.

> *The delusion that I don't need a food plan or that I can pass as a normal eater has been smashed.*

I also did some constructive self-examination that weekend. I needed to do some serious changing and growing if I was to move forward in my program of recovery. I had been acting like a baby throwing a tantrum. I wasn't putting myself down for that but rather looking at it in a healthy way. I needed to own up to how I deal with my life. I was two years in program and still whining about my food. I realized that it was time for me to grow up.

Feelings of rebellion and defiance can act themselves out in the form of dysfunctional eating behaviors, but they may have nothing to do with food. The aspirations that I had for myself, the person that I wanted to be, the things that I wanted to do, were all too big for the life I was currently living. Like the root-bound plant, I needed to re-pot myself, to give myself more room to grow.

During the weekend and the days that followed, I realized that I had just walked through a tremendously difficult time in my recovery, and, by the grace of God, I stayed abstinent through it. As much as I hadn't wanted to be willing, I had acted as if I were willing. I still had said my prayers every morning, thanking God for one more day of abstinence. I still had prayed to do God's will and not my own. I kept admitting to God that there was a part of me that didn't want to be helped. I continued to cry to God that I was in pain. I was finally brought again to my knees in willingness.

The process of surrender is astounding. Through surrender I have peace and serenity within myself again. I even started using a new scale and making accurate measurements of all my food. (The scale I was using before would sometimes stick. I could put more food on it, and it wouldn't move. Dishonesty is a big part of my disease.) Through surrender, I have begun to practice my program anew.

In the "Big Book" (paraphrased for my disease) it says that "most of us have been unwilling to admit that we were real compulsive overeaters. No person likes to think that he is bodily and mentally different from his fellows. Therefore, it is not surprising that our eating careers have been characterized by countless vain attempts to prove we could eat like other people. The idea that somehow, someday he will control and enjoy his eating is the great obsession of every abnormal eater. The persistence of this illusion is astonishing. Many pursue it to the gates of insanity or death."

During the retreat, I began to identify myself as a "real" compulsive overeater. I conceded to my innermost self that I am a compulsive overeater. The delusion that I don't need a food plan or that I can pass as a normal eater has been smashed. I know that no real compulsive overeater ever regains control, and it always takes a great deal of pain to fully understand that concept. I really put myself "out there" at the retreat that weekend by sharing at the podium every chance I got. People knew who I was; they came up to me and hugged me all weekend. I felt so loved, and I loved them all. I was known as the "real" one, and I liked that people were referring to me in that way. I am so grateful for the program of Overeaters Anonymous. It continues to save my life.

— *California USA*

Workbook Renewal

I've struggled with my abstinence my whole time in OA. When I came into the program two and a half years ago, I was on an upswing from a recent weight loss. It took me about a month to ask someone to sponsor me. She said yes and suggested I call her every day.

We set aside a time that was good for both of us. Things really began to happen after that. I worked the Steps with her and talked on the phone about everyday things that happened. I lost some weight and started to sponsor others.

The newness of it all began to wear thin, and I started slacking off on my footwork. I did everything there is to do in OA except work the Steps. My food got crazy again. I had a small weight gain, and I started to think OA didn't really work. I forgot that "it works if you work it." I went back to wanting God to take the consequences of my eating away, without taking away my compulsive overeating.

One day at a meeting someone held up an order form for a new OA publication: *The Twelve Step Workbook of Overeaters Anonymous*. Being a compulsive buyer, I had to order one. I hoped that it might give me some relief from the misery I was experiencing with my addiction.

> *I did everything there is to do in OA except work the Steps. My food got crazy again.*

I made a one-day-at-a-time commitment to work in it every day, even if I only answered one question.

When I first started using the workbook, I wanted to dig up all the stuff I used to do with food. But I found that what used to bother me no longer did. I needed to find where I was with food and my life now. So I honestly told that book what I was doing, and I saw what I was doing to myself. Then I could go on with the solution – the rest of the Steps. All of a sudden my abstinence became clearer. I started to hear again, "It works if you work it."

Every meeting I go to now, I bring up *The Twelve-Step Workbook of Overeaters Anonymous*. I tell everyone to buy one and how much it has helped me. I just can't say enough about it.

— *California USA*

After the Honeymoon

Relapse has been a part of my recovery in my six years in OA. I have no regrets — I've come to appreciate that my recovery had to be in God's time, not mine.

I came to OA with no idea what a Twelve-Step program was. I expected another diet club. That first meeting was strange — no scales to weigh in! — but the idea of a group which didn't charge dues or fees for membership was very appealing. What I heard sounded like people telling my story, and I immediately felt at home. I didn't really understand what the Steps had to do with losing weight, so I just focused on the word abstinence.

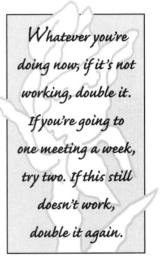

Whatever you're doing now, if it's not working, double it. If you're going to one meeting a week, try two. If this still doesn't work, double it again.

The honeymoon was wonderful. I felt such freedom being able to eat just three meals a day after being an all-day grazer and a junk-food junkie. I immediately had weight loss.

I tried to do a little "research" into whether I could try to be a normal eater again, however, and had my first relapse. The reality of a life in which I hadn't really made any changes set in. I had merely treated the OA program like a diet, and diets always come to an end. I hadn't made permanent changes in the way I live my life.

There was very little physical recovery in the young group I was attending. We were just a small group of people meeting every week and trying to figure out what a Twelve-Step program was all about. Thank God for the members who were also involved in other Twelve-Step groups who tried to help the rest of us. Thank God for guest speakers who visited our fledgling meeting to share the hope of recovery. Thank God for literature and tapes. Many times the guest speaker at a meeting was a speaker we had heard on tape. Thank God for marathons which enabled me to meet people who had been in OA for years, and who showed me recovery could be permanent.

I wanted God to zap me and make me well, and change came slowly. I've a greater respect now for the power of this disease and a greater understanding of my own powerlessness. I need to fully accept Step One, and I didn't when I first came in the door. My initial abstinence was achieved without seeking outside help. Today I realize that I can only be restored to sanity with the help of a Power greater than myself. I accepted Step Two. I finally humbled myself enough to reach out and ask for help. God has worked through the members of the group to help me achieve a long-lasting recovery.

I began working all the Steps when I realized that they had a whole lot to do with losing weight. Physical recovery was not going to remain until the Steps helped me get emotional and spiritual recovery as well. I started living my life the way the Steps have taught me. I learned to take a daily look at my actions and seek to do God's will. No longer could I try to blame, control, and fix others. I finally learned that I had to change myself.

With hindsight I see that relapse was inevitable because I wasn't willing to go to any lengths. When I was in the midst of relapse I heard another member share: "Whatever you're doing now, if it's not working, double it. If you're going to one meeting a week, try two. If you're making one phone call a day, make two. If you're reading literature for five minutes, read for ten. If all this still doesn't work, double it again."

I was finally ready to listen to the message. Today I attend four meetings a week whenever possible. I start each day reading from three daily meditation books. I take phone calls from the five people I sponsor beginning at 6:10. I call in my food plan to my sponsor. I go for walks and take time to improve my conscious contact with my Higher Power. All this has helped me to remain abstinent for two years and maintain a fifty-pound weight loss.

I'm thrilled when newcomers come to OA and get abstinent immediately. But I feel that sharing my story gives hope to anyone struggling with relapse. I tell them that what worked for me was to keep coming back. It worked when I worked it.

— *Pennsylvania USA*

Remembering the Past

I have been in OA for about nineteen years, but the major part of my recovery has occurred in the past six years. I had quit going to meetings a year or so before that, and something – my Higher Power I believe – got me back to meetings right before a health crisis in my life. The last six years have been filled with health issues and with, thankfully, a growing dependence on the program.

My way of eating has changed many times over the years, to accommodate my hypoglycemia problems, as well as my changing needs due to aging and migraines. My abstinence was sloppy at times; binges had turned to grazing, though my weight was close to normal. But I also haven't had as much peace and serenity with food as I'd longed for, even though I've worked very hard over the past few years and become more aware of my powerlessness over many things in my life.

Recently, I made a decision not to eat any of my binge foods, not even just to taste. I have been abstinent from these foods for about two months now, and the difference in the way I feel is amazing. Most of the time I feel that peace and serenity I've craved for so long. What made the difference this time? Did I finally hit bottom, again? Probably so, along with a more complete surrender – admitting that one type of food makes me crazy and gaining the willingness to try life without it. The other thing that has helped me enormously is remembering something I once saw posted in a museum.

About ten years ago, my family and I visited Dachau, the World War II concentration camp near Munich, Germany, that is open to the public. I saw many things there I will never forget, but what stays with me most is a statement by a noted philosopher that reads: "Those who cannot remember the past are condemned to repeat it."

For me that statement has come to mean that if I forget the way certain foods affect me, I will eat them again, resulting in the same crazy thoughts, actions, and cravings. Part of my new surrender has meant that I pray to my Higher Power every morning to help me remember what those foods do to me. On days when I'm confronted with especially difficult situations with food, I ask for help many times a day.

I have experienced miracles in this program, both internally and externally, and I've seen miracles happen to others. The closest friends I have are in the program, the kind of friends with whom you'd trust your life, or your children's lives, if necessary. The promises are coming true for me, slowly but surely. To newcomers and to "re-treads": keep coming back! It works if you work it!

— *Kansas USA*

"I Was Ready to Walk Out . . ."

I came into OA in November 1977. I wish I could say that I became abstinent right away, but I did not. I became abstinent in May 1996. How do I write about over eighteen years of active membership in OA? I can sum it up in two slogans: "Keep coming back, no matter what" and "Don't quit before the miracle!" After eighteen years of three meetings per week, as well as service to my group, intergroup, and region, I was ready to walk out the OA doors for the last time. I was ready to surrender to the inevitability of my disease – insanity or death. Insanity or death. But God had other plans for me.

My OA history has been characterized by periods of abstinence and longer periods of relapse, with weight swings of as much as sixty pounds every four years. I know I've said this with every relapse, but this last time was the absolute worst. I was still involved in service, continued my meeting attendance, went to new meetings in another state, worked with sponsors, prayed, had a food plan, didn't have a food plan, joined a church, became agnostic, became an atheist, and again came to believe in God. Nothing was working.

I knew I was powerless over food. I could see that my life was completely unmanageable. My spouse and I bickered constantly. My weight went up every week. I was hospitalized for suicidal depression. My alcoholic spouse became unemployed after he started drinking again. Yes, this is a progressive disease. But why couldn't I get abstinent? I'd heard OA speakers talk about people they knew who had been active and thin in OA, went back out, and had to be buried in a piano case. I would soon join that list.

Yet less than a week later, I was reminded of a promise I had made to accompany a friend to a meeting in another Twelve-Step program. Despite my grumbling, I kept my word. There they were again – those damned Twelve Steps! To make matters worse, I had to walk by the room as my OA home meeting began. All my old OA buddies were gathered around the table. How I missed them! I was back in OA a week later, but still not abstinent. My husband decided to get a six-pack one Sunday evening, and though our usual Sunday routine was to binge until we passed out, I couldn't stay home while he drank.

I have only one explanation for my return to recovery: divine intervention.

The only place I knew to go was to an OA meeting in a bordering state. I saw and heard people committed to abstinence. They had what I wanted; they gave me hope. I met someone there who was willing to guide me through my first thirty days of abstinence. We were both overwhelmed by my negativity as I struggled to follow a food plan, yet she and God and I hung in there. As I write, I am gratefully abstinent, working on a Fourth Step and looking forward to the birth of a new OA meeting in my area.

Miracles never cease. My spouse has sobered up, and my newfound abstinence is very fragile and precious to me. I pray, read literature, follow a food plan, make daily phone calls, attend at least three meetings a week, and try to offer support to my fellow OAers. I have only one explanation for my return to recovery: divine intervention. Remember: keep coming back, no matter what. And don't quit before the miracle!

— *Wyoming USA*

Part of the Journey

I've been in OA fifteen years, and although relapse is something I would never have asked for in a million years, it's been a major factor in my incredible recovery.

Relapse was my greatest fear whenever I got close to goal weight. My fear of success would tell me: "I've never been able to maintain my weight before, so why should this time be any different?"

I sabotaged myself with lies and illusions I picked up from people in my past. It never occurred to me that these thoughts were their opinions, not facts or reality.

Working the Steps and using the tools have been my insurance against another relapse. But it's not a guarantee. I work my program just as diligently, if not more so, than when I started my losing abstinence a year ago. I'm now at maintenance, working hard on emotional recovery.

My spiritual program has been the foundation of my recovery. My Higher Power, whom I choose to call God, is constantly present in my life. What I have today wouldn't be possible without the presence of God. This relationship is helping me reclaim self-love, hope, and faith.

I gained sixty pounds after my divorce and lived in relapse for two years. I was crushed, humiliated, and ashamed that my second marriage had failed. I was sure it was because of me, so I dived headlong into my disease.

"No one will hurt me anymore," I told myself. "I'm tired of being used and tossed aside. I'll never care for anyone ever again." Self-pity and pain ruled my life.

But I never stopped going to meetings. The love and acceptance of the Fellowship kept drawing me back week after week. It was the only family that really cared about me. I knew that the answer to my emptiness was in OA.

In relapse I learned just how bad my disease of compulsive overeating can get. This last one put me at my top weight of two hundred pounds. Movement became more and more difficult; I couldn't lift my leg in the shower or move over in bed without rolling. My legs and feet hurt just from everyday walking. But, most of all, the great distance between me and my God was a deep, yearning ache. I felt as if I'd die inside if I didn't begin to reclaim God's presence in my life.

Somewhere inside me there stirred a spark: a longing to be with people, to learn how to trust so I could make friends. I began to yearn for the friendship and intimacy of a man. Most of all, I wanted my peace of mind back, that precious serenity. And I knew that before any of this would be possible, physical recovery was necessary.

The school year began and God came alive inside me. I surrendered again, committing my life and will to the care of God. I got a sponsor and partner in recovery. The Steps and tools became my life. I did another Fourth-Step inventory, and my character defects jumped off the pages. I could no longer deny my arrogance, self-righteousness, and judgmental attitude. The meaning of Step Two was revealed to me as never before, and I understood humility.

None of this would have been possible without the relapse. Why? Because I saw how bad the disease could get. The disease taught me that I never want to be that sick and lonely again. It taught me to never again lose my identity to a man or live in the lies and illusions of the past.

Today my life is rich with real friends in the OA Fellowship. I'm finding the courage to feel the feelings, and I'm beginning new friendships with both men and women. That's very risky for me, because it involves shedding my mask, being open, honest, and most of all, trusting.

I'm dancing and dating again. I simply wouldn't be able to allow my sexuality to flower without God and the support and love I've found in OA. I don't reject or deny relapse as some awful mistake; I embrace it as part of my recovery journey. I can see how God has always been there for me.

— *Washington USA*

Final Surrender

I had three wonderful years of abstinence after I came into OA in 1978. I was on top of the world. Then, like a rug being pulled out from underneath, I found myself back into compulsive overeating.

For nine long and agonizingly painful years, I continued in my disease. Not knowing what happened or why, I wondered what I had done wrong, but I found no answers.

I didn't give up on OA, but I didn't always go to meetings since it was too painful to see people who had abstinence. I continued to work the Steps as best I could, and I read OA literature and kept in touch with other non-abstaining OA members. We gave each other comfort and support in our pain.

During those nine long years, I was confused and angry at myself and God. I had my nose rubbed into my character defects until I not only recognized but accepted them. Dishonesty, lying, cheating, and stealing were all part of my compulsion to eat. I wore the seven deadly sins on my chest. I felt the pain of child-hood which I had kept locked inside. But once I owned up to my defects, I humbled myself and it felt good. I drew closer to my Higher Power. I prayed long and hard for faith in God and in recovery. I prayed for a spiritual experience. I prayed for help with my disease.

And God answered me. My eyes were opened and all the things I didn't accept when I first came to OA I now understood and accepted wholeheartedly. I accepted that I have a disease – compulsive overeating – that I am bodily and mentally different from other people, and that I have to take responsibility for my care.

I surrendered my will. It's no pink-cloud situation, but it's a fact of life which I accept and feel comfortable with. My compulsion has been lifted and sanity has returned. I realize my disease will flare up now and again. When it does, I'll just have to take my medicine.

— *Utah USA*

"I Lost Sight of What Moderate Was . . ."

When most people talk about relapse, they mean a break in abstinence, or leaving the program. I have experienced a type of relapse that I have not heard many people talk about. I have gained a lot of weight while still being completely abstinent, going to meetings, and doing service.

My first year in the program, I lost about fifty pounds. I am five feet, one inch tall, and I went down to 117 pounds. I thought my goal weight should be 112, because I weighed that for about ten minutes when I was twenty-three years old. Fourteen years later, I became quite ill – I came down with what is now called Chronic Fatigue Syndrome, and at the time was referred to as Epstein-Barr virus. The bottom line was that I was not eating enough to stay healthy.

What I've had the least experience with is maintaining a healthy weight.

I never thought I would experience the anorexic side of the disease, but I did. I derived pleasure out of seeing how little I could eat and still call it a meal. When I got sick, I had to change many things, but I only started feeling better after I had gained back some of my weight. I believe I'm healthy at around 125 to 130 pounds, but I kept gaining weight.

I've had lots of experience in my life gaining weight, and quite a bit losing weight. What I've had the least experience with is maintaining a healthy weight. Once I began gaining weight, I lost sight of what "moderate" was, and most of my meals included "calorie-dense" or rich foods. I know how to pack the most into a meal! I found recreation, comfort, and entertainment in my meals, and I kept on gaining weight. I also realized that I had been using coffee and diet soda to get me from one meal to the next, and I let go of them shortly after my second OA birthday. That was a difficult adjustment.

When I talked to people at meetings, they told me that I

looked fine. I know now that they were uncomfortable with the subject. I often see people now who are experiencing what I did, and I approach them. I tell them, as lovingly as I can, that I can see they've put on some weight. I tell them that I gained weight in abstinence and that I had a lot of shame about it, that I couldn't find anyone to talk to who understood what I was going through. I give them my phone number and tell them that I would welcome their call. I do the same with people that I see who are awfully thin.

I believe we can still practice our disease in abstinence. Most of us who are "maintainers" do experience some weight fluctuation at some point. We have to learn to eat abstinently and moderately a day at a time, for the rest of our lives. I didn't stop being a compulsive eater the day I became abstinent; I was just able to refrain from acting on my thoughts and wishes about food, with the help of my Higher Power.

I had a lot of shame about my weight gain. I felt very alone. I would attend a meeting and feel like everyone else was in the room, and I was way out in the parking lot. I didn't know what to do. Several things helped me: one was a committed Step-study meeting where we go through the Steps, take a break for a few weeks, and then start again. Another thing that really renewed my passion for recovery was when we got our own OA "Twelve and Twelve."

I do a written Tenth Step every night. For years I would write, "I pray for the willingness to eat moderately." That willingness did come, but gradually. In my ninth and tenth years of abstinence I was able to let go of the excess weight – another example of not quitting before the miracle happens. I'm very grateful that I could trust that the right body would show up, that I just needed to keep working my program. Now the challenge, once again, is to maintain a healthy weight. I certainly have more tools than I did eight years ago, but I know I can't do it alone.

— *California USA*

Sold on Recovery

Finding OA is the best thing that ever happened to me. I'm very grateful to someone special who told me about this wonderful program. I wanted what she had. In my case, "attraction, rather than promotion" really worked.

I went to my first OA meeting in July of 1981. I weighed two hundred pounds and felt very fat, ugly, and depressed. I could relate to everything that was said, and I knew I was home.

I didn't talk much that first year, but I paid attention at every meeting. I ate three meals a day and lost forty pounds. Although I had trouble maintaining a consistent abstinence, I never gave up hope.

On July 6, 1986 my husband and I went away for a weekend. While he went to a baseball game, I went to a mall to shop for the day. I started with one compulsive bite and was gone. I ate all day and felt as if I'd gotten away with something. At home again, however, I told my sponsor:

I'm either going to work this program one hundred percent, or I know I'm going to be three hundred pounds.

"This is it. I'm either going to work this program one hundred percent, or I know I'm going to be three hundred pounds." I committed to three meals a day and calling my sponsor daily.

I've lost seventy-seven pounds, going from a size-twenty to a size-five dress, and have stayed the same weight for four years. I weigh myself only once a year at my doctor's office.

There have been so many miracles in my life. I have a great relationship with my HP. I have a beautiful marriage and a supportive husband. I've learned to tell him everything, even how I feel. My family and in-laws have also been very supportive. One special memory I have is of the Christmas when I had lost fifty pounds. My brother said that he, as well as everyone else in my family, was very proud of me – and they all clapped for me. It meant so much and brought tears to my eyes.

In OA I feel I have found the answer to my life. I have an illness. At thirty years of age I'm the happiest I've ever been. To stay that way I have to maintain my conscious contact with God. As long as I have my abstinence, peace, and serenity, I have everything.

I want to thank all of the very special friends I have made in OA over the last nine years. They have helped and inspired me so much. As long as I keep doing what I'm doing every day and work with my sponsor, I'll stay in recovery. If I can do it, so can you. So "Keep coming back, and don't leave before the miracle happens!"

— *Wisconsin USA*

A Cunning Compulsion

While writing an article for our intergroup newsletter, I used the well-known program phrase "cunning, baffling, and powerful."

> *It wasn't until I became abstinent and saw all of my life-threatening physical problems disappear in ninety days that I realized how completely I'd deluded myself.*

I was struck by the word "cunning," so I looked it up, using my word processor's thesaurus program. Here are some of the synonyms I found:

1. Canny. Even after several months of strong abstinence, I am amazed at how persistent and subtle my compulsion's inner voice can be. "You couldn't reach your sponsor to commit your food today, so you can eat that extra piece without feeling guilty."

The other day I was in the lunchroom at work, alone with a basket of sweets someone had baked. In the first few seconds after I noticed the basket, at least ten different tempting thoughts went through my head. Excuses, rationalizations, you name it – as though each thought had been calculated by my eating disorder for maximum effect.

2. Crafty. My disease puts me into difficult emotional and physical situations. It's as if my "food thing" knows that if I become too tired or stressed, I'll be more likely to break my abstinence. Some nights I find myself unable to go to sleep for no discernible reason – until suddenly food thoughts attack me. Something inside my compulsive mind purposely makes me tired enough to be receptive.

3. Deceptive. The program word for this is denial. I remember thinking, in the last few horrible months of my relapse before I returned to OA: "Throwing up in the morning is no big thing. It's probably the amount of stress I'm under at work. Job stress explains my poor immune system, too. And my family has a history of diabetes and high blood pressure, so that's why I have those two problems."

I honestly believed that my overeating had nothing to do with my poor health. It wasn't until I became abstinent and saw all of my life-threatening physical problems disappear in ninety days that I realized how completely I'd deluded myself.

4. Shrewd. Since I came back into OA, I've had to be very careful with the practical details of my abstinence. I follow a definite food plan. Every night I write down my food for the next day and call it into my sponsor. Despite all my precautions, though, my eating disorder constantly leads me to look for loopholes.

For instance, I recently had to start weighing and measuring even noncaloric items like artificial sweeteners, spices, and salt. I found that once I was thoroughly committed to planning my daily food, my eating disorder would cause me to overestimate the amounts needed to flavor my food. The old thinking that said "if a little is good, a lot is better" caused me to over-salt my food and put a dozen sweetener packets into my iced tea.

I didn't have much success with abstinence until I was willing to commit myself to weighing and measuring everything. I was unable to resist finding those loopholes – the little extra "healthy" food – which would inevitably lead to a binge on greasy fast food.

5. Wily. Recovery is an honest way of living. My compulsion, on the other hand, constantly prompts me to be dishonest and

tricky. Over the years, I've mastered every trick for sneak eating: fluffing up the remaining food in a bowl so that no one can tell I've eaten any of it; slipping out at 1:00 a.m. to buy binge foods while my husband slept; buying a reversible jacket so I could sneak sweets into the house in the inside pockets. I've lied to coworkers, sponsors, and friends, even when there was no reason to be dishonest.

Once I almost choked to death at a turnpike rest area trying to stuff down some vending machine junk while my husband was in the bathroom. My husband wouldn't have objected to my eating. But my sick, compulsive mind knew that I couldn't possibly order a large enough lunch in public to satisfy my addiction, so I was doing a little "padding" beforehand.

Since my return to OA last spring I've been blessed with solid and honest abstinence. For the most part, my compulsion to overeat has been lifted. I'm still tormented, however, by binge thoughts and rationalizations at unexpected moments. Don't take this illness lightly. I have to make abstinence my first priority, because if even one of those cunning thoughts hits home, I'll lose everything, including my life.

— *Delaware USA*

CHAPTER FIVE

"I know now why I relapsed..."

Members share the lessons they learned
during their relapse experiences.

No Graduation Day

I know now why relapse has been a part of my OA history. I never fully admitted to myself that I was a compulsive overeater. I was either unwilling or unready to make the changes necessary for continuous abstinence and recovery.

I was twenty-one and weighed 310 pounds when I walked through the doors of my first OA meeting a little over five years ago. I was down from my top weight of 350, having just gone off a diet on which I'd lost about forty pounds. I'd been told about OA by a recovering bulimic and alcoholic, and I talked to her about it for at least a week before I went to my first meeting.

> *I was either unwilling or unready to make the changes necessary for continuous abstinence and recovery.*

At that time I was very proud to say that I was already abstinent. I had this program figured out, and I hadn't been near a meeting yet! This attitude destined me for a relapse before I even got started.

I went to meetings, gave up a lot of foods, and lost a lot of weight. I identified certain foods as problems for me – but I thought that one day I'd have enough recovery under my belt to grab the brass ring and graduate from OA. I didn't fully believe that I'd never recover; I hadn't hit bottom.

My first relapse occurred sometime after my one-year anniversary in OA. I'd lost at least one hundred pounds, but I'd slowly begun taking back some of my binge foods. I had stopped going to meetings regularly. I didn't have a sponsor.

There was little recovery in local meetings and no one willing to be a sponsor. This was a good excuse for me not to have one. Besides, I thought I had what it took to make it on my own: abstinence, weight loss, and OA literature. Needless to say, I was in relapse within a few months.

It was hell. Relapse was worse than my pre-OA days, because now I knew what I was doing to myself! Before program I could be sickeningly oblivious.

I felt fear, pain, and despair. I knew that if I continued to eat, I'd gain all the weight back. I knew that without OA meetings and the other tools, I couldn't recover. But getting back to meetings was like pulling teeth. I had to be in enough pain to go back, and about five months later, I finally was.

I was still into the food. I didn't work the Steps or get a sponsor. Then my Higher Power did something miraculous for me and the other OA members in our town by sending us a recovering OA member from California. She immediately began sponsoring people and sharing her recovery. I began talking to one of this woman's sponsorees on the phone every morning, and when she herself became a sponsor, I became her first sponsoree.

I worked through all the Steps with her. I made some amends. I was abstinent, and I lost more weight. By the end of that summer, I was down to 156 pounds, and I thought I'd finally gotten it. By the end of September, I quit going to so many meetings, stopped working Steps Ten and Eleven, took back some food, and put on ten pounds.

That fall I started sponsoring people. This reinforced the idea that I had it made. I could now tell others how to work their programs. I was obviously "Miss OA" – and so began my second relapse.

By August of the next year I ceased sponsoring anybody. I was angry at God, not attending meetings regularly, and overeating – controlled eating rather than bingeing. These periods of control and weight loss fostered my denial. I told myself I really wasn't doing that badly – I just needed to read a little more and work a little harder to get back the abstinence I had before.

In my diseased mind, I developed the notion that it was all right for me to eat most foods as long as I stuck with three meals a day and nothing in between. I grabbed fat serenity and held on tight, believing that if I were spiritually fit, I could eat anything I wanted to.

For the next couple of years, my weight fluctuated between 165 and 180. I thought this was maintenance. By early 1991, I'd dropped in and out of OA so many times I'd lost count. I gave up most of my OA support system and went through another relapse during which I gained fifty pounds in less than five months.

This shocked and appalled me. I kept telling myself, "I've got to get back into OA." In the early part of this year, after almost four more months of hell, I finally did.

I began calling in my food to a new sponsor in February. I was eating better and lost some weight, but I didn't ask her for any ideas or feedback. I still thought I knew what was best for me and didn't want anybody to prove me wrong.

> *It's a lot easier to prevent a relapse than it is to get out of one.*

In early April I consciously took back the food in order to get through a crisis – a new job and a major geographical move. I went through it all overeating and fogged. I was lonely, miserable, and hopeless and felt that everything I'd ever done in OA was wrong. I realized my ideas didn't work, and I needed help. After five years of hearing about how I needed OA, I finally knew that I did.

I came back to OA, and a wonderful surprise was waiting for me. There were so many meetings filled with recovery, abstinence, hope, and sponsors! When I was really ready to hear the truth, the truth was there to be heard at OA meetings.

I started dragging myself to those meetings, going to one a day for almost a month. Now I average three or four times a week. I realized that in order to hear what I hadn't heard before, I had to make myself available to hear it.

In early June I got a new sponsor who has the "black-and-white" abstinence that I was yearning for and now have. It's simple. Either I'm abstinent or I'm not. There is no sloppy eating. There are no slips. If I choose to eat what I don't eat in recovery, I've chosen to give up my abstinence. I'm grateful to say that today I don't make that choice.

Yesterday I celebrated thirty days of a clean and beautiful abstinence. I didn't think it could happen, but it did. How lucky I am to have found OA, and how grateful I am to be in it!

During most of my days in OA, I didn't allow anyone to smack me in the face with the reality of this disease – and I doubt I could have listened if anyone did. I've since come to believe that it's a chronic, progressive, and deadly disease that has no cure.

There's more to relapse than just weight gain. Included in the package are despair, hopelessness, guilt, remorse, shame, and fear. It's a lot easier to prevent a relapse than it is to get out of one.

I know my recovery will last if I'm willing to do a few simple things: abstain daily from those foods that hurt me; go to as many meetings as I can; be honest; work toward humility; listen to my sponsor and do what she says. If I do these things, I'll never have to go back into relapse again.

— *Connecticut USA*

Opening My Eyes

I thought someone might still be working, so I entered from the front door. As I turned the key I quickly darted my eyes left, then right, looking for any sign of movement.

"Security, anybody working?" I said loudly. If anyone had been working, I would say I was there for a security purpose. I went around the office quickly, repeating this, impatient to get what I wanted.

I wasn't there for any security purpose. I was there for the same reason I always entered the suites: to steal food, to binge and not pay for it. So far I'd been pretty lucky, but my luck ran out that night.

I rounded the corner and entered the kitchen. They had really laid out a spread this time. I hastily devoured what I could see and checked the fridge. I looked through the cabinet, too, but that was just force of habit, like going to a stranger's bathroom and checking the medicine cabinet.

It had become routine for me. I'd been doing it since the very first day I was hired. I forgot that taking food from another suite meant automatic termination, not to mention that it was immoral and unfair to the food's owner. I was in relapse, and this was a free ride.

The next day I was shown a tape of myself stealing food and was fired. Looking back I'd had a sneaking feeling that they had finally installed a camera to catch the food thief. But I couldn't stop myself. The food called me as clearly as if Cindy Crawford had beckoned.

> *The food is really the last thing to go. I was in relapse long before I picked up the food.*

I'd been slipping with the food long before that incident. But being fired really woke me up. I'd always been pretty secure that no matter how bad the food got, at least I wasn't an addict who couldn't hold down a job. But I could no longer deny what I had been doing, and I saw how terrible a relapse I'd been through.

I'd been lying to my sponsor for some time. I'm grateful that I managed to be honest with him. I decided to go back to school, and I start a new job next week. I feel better about myself. Doing the things that got me sick won't help me get well, so a lot of things about my behavior, in and out of meetings, has changed also.

One thing that contributed to my food debacle was "thirteenth stepping." I never took advantage of anyone, but I think that I would have. I was looking at sick young women, fairly new to program, for dates. "Come over to my place and we'll talk program!" It wasn't the program I had on my mind.

Today I go to meetings to recover. I'm going to ninety meetings in ninety days, and when I go to a meeting it stays a meeting for me. It used to be that once a pretty woman walked into the room it wasn't a meeting anymore, it was a social club. I'm working this program harder than ever. I realize that the food is really the last thing to go. I was in relapse long before I picked up the food.

— *Illinois USA*

Footwork

The other day a friend and I were sitting on a park bench. She was saying that her food was out of control. She was going to pray for the willingness to become abstinent.

> *Each meal began with the Third-Step prayer. I became abstinent with God's help.*

A memory flashed into my mind: Spring, 1986, down by the duck pond. My sponsor was discussing abstinence with me. I'd been in program for about a month and was struggling with my food plan. She was trying to explain how abstinence was achieved.

"You need to pray for the willingness to place abstinence above the short-term gratification of food. Abstinence is a gift given by God. Ask God for abstinence, and it will be given to you."

I went home and prayed to God for the willingness to become abstinent. Apparently God was out of abstinence. I wasn't given the gift.

After reporting God's failure to grant my request, my sponsor sat me down to explain the facts of life. She brought out *For Today.* Turning to May 15, she read: "Pray to God, but continue to row to shore." She explained to me what that line meant. I wasn't supposed to just pray to God and expect results. I was supposed to pray for the energy to be abstinent and put effort into the process. I was to be an active partner. She quoted another saying, "Pray as though everything depended on God, and act as though everything depended on you."

She told me that prayer would work if I put muscle into it. To protect myself from the impulse of breaking my abstinence, prayer was most effective if done away from the food. I had to put the fork down first and then enlist God's help. Somehow the desire to be abstinent was stronger when my hands were folded in my lap instead of wrapped around a fork.

This technique worked. Each meal began with the Third-Step prayer. I became abstinent with God's help. I was rowing to shore.

Back in the present I turned to my friend with a smile. "My sponsor told me to pray to God, but continue to row to shore. Let me tell you how it works."

— *Wisconsin USA*

I'll Never Trade Serenity

I am abstinent today. It is hard to be grateful as I look in the mirror and see my weight gain. It's hard, as I try to find something in my closet that will fit around my seventy-pound weight gain. But I am abstinent today.

> *How could I have traded in the precious gift of abstinence – the serenity and wholeness – for a Twinkie®?*

Relapse is hell. After over four years of abstinence, I guess I needed more research to prove I was a compulsive overeater. I forgot that a lifetime of morbid obesity had robbed me of a full life. How could I have taken for granted the precious gift of abstinence that had ushered in serenity and wholeness? How could I have traded that in for a Twinkie®? Yes, I know I have a disease, but I decided I could be a "social eater." After all, I had maintained my weight loss with "just a little more" here and there. I insisted that I still looked good; I'd convinced myself that I was graduating from being "Mr. OA" to "Mr. Normal Eater." I thought that maybe I'd made too big a deal of this abstinence business, which led me right into the abyss of relapse.

How does a person gain fifty pounds in five months? A compulsive overeater like me does it easily. The disease had been waiting inside me for an opportunity to rise up in destructive eating. I was soon aware of the reality of my relapse, but that was not enough for me to stop. I kept looking for the next binge that would be the last one. I was lost in the hopelessness of isolation with all the old foods, filling myself up, but feeling more and more empty inside.

What had gone wrong? As a result of a strong spiritual base grounded in my Higher Power's gift of abstinence, I had added too much to my agenda of living. I had a life that was full of commitments and goals, but they started crowding in on my program. There was less time for meetings, less time for reading OA literature, less time for addressing my feelings through writing, and, most important, less time to seek God and the knowledge of God's will for my life. I was in charge again, and compulsive eating was my antidote for the failure.

For today, I am back. I have had periods of abstinence, then slips, then breaks, then the hopelessness that compels me back to our program of recovery. Where else does a compulsive overeater like me belong? I do not have to explain myself to you, my OA brothers and sisters. You know me because we share the same disease. You have loved me and encouraged me, and I have needed to hear your suggestions.

I've added a second sponsor and am starting a new adventure into the Twelve Steps. I've started therapy to deal with unresolved childhood issues. I am committed to abstinence one day at a time. I must put the relapse behind me, remembering that I am a beloved child of God – even with seventy more pounds. I'm learning humility and am grateful for abstinence this day. I am back home!

— *Texas USA*

A NEW BEGINNING 103

Still Powerless

For those of us who have spent many years being overweight, the idea of "goal weight" has a nearly magical allure. Like anything long-sought and elusive, goal weight has been invested with images, dreams, and hopes. Even when we learn that recovery is not just a matter of losing weight, we cannot help but remain attached to the idea of being at our most desirable weight.

I officially reached goal weight two weeks ago. My immediate thinking was that I was now ready for a "maintenance" food plan as opposed to the basic eating plan I had been following. "Maintenance plan" held an allure similar to "goal weight" because it suggested the promise of more food. This reaction – seeing goal weight and maintenance in terms of what additional food I would get to eat – should have been a warning signal, but I did not see it as such.

So I happily began a maintenance plan, adding one serving of a specified food per day to my menu. Much of the week I concentrated on this one additional serving of food, obsessing about when I would eat it, what it would be, and what it would do to me. When I weighed myself the next week I found I had gained a pound, which unnerved me. Several hours later, I relapsed for the first time in nine months.

What had happened? Why is it that for nine months I had been free from the desire to eat compulsively and then, within one week of reaching my goal, had relapsed? As I contemplated my slip and talked to my sponsor and my OA friends, I realized that the slip had started well before the actual moment when I ate the food. I realized that my whole conception of goal weight and maintenance was ill-formed, bearing more resemblance to my disease than my recovery. The more this poorly formed conception directed me, the farther I got from true recovery. And when I removed myself from recovery, I relapsed.

When I first began practicing a serious, daily program of recovery, I understood very quickly and intuitively that I did not have to think about, worry about, or "figure out" losing weight. Although I used a food plan and committed my food daily to my sponsor, I did this in order to surrender and help quiet my compulsive mind.

Once I had surrendered my food, I was free to read literature, write, share at meetings, and support other compulsive overeaters. The more my energy went into developing a relationship with my Higher Power and working the Steps of the program, the less I thought about my weight. I did not worry about how long it would take me to lose weight; I trusted completely that as my recovery progressed, my body would heal. On a daily basis I felt better in every way: spiritually enlivened, emotionally calmer, and physically healthier.

When I reached goal weight, however, my attention suddenly turned to weight and food issues. It was only after my relapse that I grasped that maintenance is no more about maintaining weight than recovery is about losing weight. By being so focused on weight and food during my first week of maintenance, I had returned to thinking patterns associated with my disease. I had not focused on a spiritual and sane life, nor had I surrendered to my Higher Power. Instead I had started to act as if I had to exert a great deal of control in order to manage my weight. It was this very effort at control that led me to relapse.

> *My whole conception of goal weight and maintenance was ill-formed, bearing more resemblance to my disease than my recovery.*

It is bemusing to me that I could slip back into denial so easily. Who was I to think that I could control my eating at goal weight any better than I had been able to when overweight? During nine months of recovery, I had entrusted my life to my Higher Power and had reaped more rewards than I could begin to recount here. In one week of maintenance, I suddenly thought I was in charge, and the disease was instantly reactivated. I am grateful for my relapse because it allowed me to see myself clearly and to get back to the business of working my program. Not a special food-oriented program for maintenance, but a basic program that involves nutritional, emotional, and spiritual components. I do the footwork, and my Higher Power takes care of everything else.

— *Washington USA*

The Queen Abdicates

After two years of working a very strong program, I felt as if I'd be able to deal with any change, feeling, or event abstinently. I had faithfully attended meetings. I had a sponsor. I wrote, meditated, did service. I'd dedicated my life to God and to OA.

Eight weeks ago I had a huge wedding. I not only got married, but I changed jobs, names, credit cards, and responsibilities. I left home and am now a fifteen-hour drive away. Being from a very close, supportive, yet codependent family, this last proved most difficult and trying.

As soon as we moved, I dove into OA. I immediately got a sponsor, attended as many meetings as I could, and admitted my loneliness and neediness at meetings. But I still felt empty. I wanted to feel whole, like I had with my old group and sponsor, and I wanted it now!

I couldn't understand these feelings. And to think that people used to call me the "Queen of Change"! Surely change alone couldn't be causing this confusion and this deep void inside me. Slowly but surely I started to forget how utterly powerless I am over food. I experimented and slipped three times. I'd thought those days were over. "Where'd that come from?" I asked. "I can deal with change, can't I? What's up?"

> I'm human, and I made a mistake. I'm not perfect, and I really don't want to be.

After a period of anger and disappointment with myself, I can honestly say I've forgiven myself for those slips. Even though my compulsive mind says I gained weight and need to start over, I know I'm still at my maintenance weight, and I don't need to give up any of the recovery I've had until now. I'm human, and I made a mistake. I'm not perfect, and I really don't want to be. I know now that I'm powerless over change as well as food.

I feel extremely humble today. I've gone back to the first three Steps. I'm grateful that God brought me through, because I don't want to return to hell. I surrender my will and life to God completely, one day at a time. Food no longer works. It can't solve anything, and turning to it can no longer be a choice in my life. If I want to live, I need to be grateful to God for what I've survived. I'm also grateful to my fellow OAers. Because of you, I have a place I can go. I choose life, and, God willing, I'll keep coming back.

— *Texas USA*

Abstinence as Result

Today I celebrated another day of abstinence. This makes about five years of freedom from overeating for me. But I didn't begin OA five years ago; I began nine years ago. What was I doing during those first four years?

When I came to OA, I was completely defeated from this disease, and my soul was just about dead. It felt as though there was absolutely no end in sight. And there probably would have been no end, except that I kept coming back. I was encouraged by my fellow members to work the program by going to meetings, using the other tools and studying Steps One, Two, and Three.

Abstinence in OA was not one of the first things I experienced. What I did experience right away was a halt in the progression of the disease. Once I started to do the things I was encouraged to do, this disease never got any worse for me. That in itself was a miracle.

I'm very grateful to my fellow members who always encouraged me to keep doing what I was doing. I never felt ashamed because I could not completely stay away from overeating all the time. Also I never felt I wasn't qualified to work the Steps. I was always aware that what I was doing in OA – using the tools, working the Steps – was better than what I was doing before I came to OA, which was nothing at all. If I had waited to become abstinent in this program in order to work the Steps, I'm sure that I would not be writing this today.

Eventually, the time came when I could and did abstain from

overeating completely. This was a result of the first three Steps of the program, particularly Step Three. It's no coincidence that I was able to make a clean break from the food at the same time I was working Step Three. That's because I spent more time focusing on God, and I had less time to focus on food. At the same time that I was learning that I needed God in my life, I was learning that I no longer needed excess food.

These days, when I meet members who feel discouraged because they feel they're doing everything but abstaining, I share my experience and remind them that, for some of us, abstinence comes as a result.

— *Anonymous*

Relapse Revelations

Two weeks ago I gave in to the compulsion to overeat, and I've been in a major relapse ever since. I'm by no means happy about this, but looking back, I've learned a lot of lessons I hope I'll never forget.

• I can no longer allow myself the luxury of a "one-day" binge. My illness has progressed far beyond that point.

• When I'm in relapse there's never enough food. I run frantically from sweet to salty, from cold to hot, and start the cycle all over again — never finding that one elusive "magic" food that will sedate me at last. I'm like a wild woman, cramming down food well past the point of feeling sick and stuffed — yet already planning what to eat next.

• The food I binged on didn't do one thing to make me feel better. All it did was steal two weeks of my life.

• When I'm in relapse, I become so obsessed that I can think of nothing else. Each evening is spent planning my binges for the next day, wrestling with the compulsion monster far into the night, wondering: "Will I binge tomorrow? What will I binge on? How will I sneak the food? Where will I hide the wrappers?" Even in sleep the obsession controls me.

• When I give in to the food, my disease rapidly reactivates. I find myself behaving as destructively as I did in my pre-OA days – waking up each morning thinking: "This is it! I'm going to be okay today"– only to find myself diving desperately for the food just a few hours later.

• I haven't forgotten how to be sneaky. I caught myself secretly eating large amounts of food when no one was around, then hiding the trash. What I had forgotten was the tremendous amount of guilt and self-hatred that go along with that behavior. When I'm sneak-eating, I feel like a phony while my true self gets lost under mounds of food and negative behavior.

> Perhaps the most important realization that's come out of this is that I do know how to surrender after all.

But perhaps the most important realization that's come out of this is that I do know how to surrender after all. I always questioned the concept of surrendering to a Higher Power. But now I see that for the past two weeks I totally surrendered to food! I'd given food complete control and power over me. I was no longer in charge of my life or how I spent my time; the obsession decided that for me.

Since I already know what it means to give something complete power over me, why not surrender to what will truly care for me and love me as food never can: a loving Higher Power that I choose to call God?

As I've heard said so many times, and now truly believe: "It's much harder to get abstinent than to stay abstinent" and "Nothing tastes as good as abstinence feels."

— *Florida USA*

Just a Little Won't Hurt

As I slowly came out of relapse and back into abstinence, I asked my Higher Power to help me remember to stay close to the spiritual self that abstinence gives me. When in relapse, my spirit is sick, sad, and guilt-ridden. I wonder why I hurt myself like this. When I am abstinent, I wonder how I could hurt myself in the first place by taking that first bite into relapse.

It's been a very difficult year in my life. Why did I think the sedation of a little extra food wouldn't hurt? I thought I needed it. I thought it would be okay this time. I thought I could control it this time. Just once, I thought, like everybody else. Can you hear the disease? Can you read the cunning and powerful seduction?

> *I thought I could control it this time. Just once, I thought, like everybody else.*

All it did for me was let my body take back thirty pounds of hard-won weight loss. More significantly, it tortured my soul with its vicious recrimination as I struggled with it.

What saved me was that I never left OA. I kept coming back. I listened to OA Twelve-Step tapes as I drifted off to sleep. I read the "Big Book." I knew I had to work the program in every way. Yes, even in relapse I knew OA was my only chance at relieving my food addiction.

The situations of my life haven't changed, but I am abstinent now. I am dealing with the same problems over which I have no control, but my spirit is free. I am clear about not hurting myself today, right now, this minute.

Thank you, Higher Power, for today's abstinence and for pulling me as I reached.

— *Anonymous*

Looking Good Isn't Enough

Mine is a familiar OA story of desperation, hope, recovery, desperation, hope, and recovery. You see, I am one who lost weight in the program, relapsed, and now have a true program and a new abstinence and weight loss.

I thought this program was too weird and crazy for me when I first came to meetings. I thought it was a program for lazy women and men who did not know how to control themselves. Never mind that I weighed over four hundred pounds; I was in control and did not belong here.

I left for four months, and when I came back, I tried to believe I was one of these people. I think that was my downfall, because I still thought that these people were just what I used to think they were. My shame made me take the First Step and admit that I was one of them – a lazy person with no self-control.

I started the program with a sick mind, and I worked it in a sick way. I enjoyed a great success in my first year; with my doctor looking over my shoulder, I lost all my excess weight. I was down to 190 pounds and feeling great. Or so I thought. This disease can be very deceiving.

Soon I was too busy for my OA friends, my wife, or anything other than looking good. As a fat person, my whole life had been so negative. So, when I started getting positive attention for my appearance, I didn't know how to handle it.

I was on the speaking circuit, making the rounds to meetings, showing off the new me. I began to think I could control my eating. After all, I'd lost over two hundred pounds! I must be stronger than the rest of you. After my divorce, my new-and-improved life didn't look so good anymore. I started eating again – not bingeing, but gradually putting more and more on my plate.

I started going to fewer meetings. And so my downward spiral began. Before it was over, I'd gained fifty-five pounds. I thought: "How did I get back here? I followed the program, dammit! I lost two hundred pounds! This can't happen to me." The shame that followed was the worst I'd ever felt in my life.

I went to a meeting and called my sponsor. I'd only spoken to him once in eight months. And then something strange happened to me. I went to meetings with my mouth shut and my ears open. I listened to everyone, to everything they said. I no longer wanted to be the class star; I just wanted to find the answers. I got a new "Big Book" and started over again. I read the "Big Book" and let it really sink in. Most importantly, I found and believed in a Higher Power.

I learned that I am not weak-willed. I have the disease of compulsive overeating. That is what I am. I will never be cured. I can use the Twelve Steps and Twelve Traditions to learn how to live with my disease – how to live fully and happily. As a sick person takes medication to stay alive, I must take the program as a way to live freely and happily.

I went to a meeting one evening and pitched about relapse and felt a love and understanding I never thought possible. I was asked to speak about it at other meetings. I've found that many know the shame of relapse, but few are willing to talk about it openly. They feel as though they failed. I, for one, am grateful for my relapse; it taught me what the program is about. It brought me to my knees and gave me the way to find a program, an abstinent way of living, that I will follow for the rest of my life.

I feel great today. I have lost twenty of the fifty-five pounds I'd gained, and my goal weight is in sight. This time, I know who is responsible for my success. My Higher Power and OA top the list. My name is not even on the list this time. I have been blessed with opportunities to share my story with people in relapse, letting them know that they are not alone. If you are in relapse, I hope you can feel some of the hope that I feel for the future.

No matter who you are – whether you are new or struggling or have a great program – I want to encourage you to share your program. Share with your mate, your sponsor, a friend. Share yourself. You will find that the more you share, the more you gain. And keep coming back. We love you, and we'll always understand.

— *Anonymous*

Without Exception

I tried all sorts of different ways to control my compulsive overeating: shots, pills, hypnosis, liquid diets, laxatives, and diet clubs. I finally came to OA during the holidays of 1985.

After that first OA meeting I thought: "There's no way I'm going to give up the food until after the holidays." I came back for a second meeting and became abstinent the next day, January 1, 1986.

I was told to read the "Big Book," come to meetings, work the Twelve Steps and use all the tools. I was so tired of failing in my battle to lose weight, but I was willing to try one last time.

"Abstinence is the most important thing in my life today without exception," became my personal motto, and I would say it at all the meetings. I did everything I was told. I followed a food plan with which I was comfortable. I gave up white flour and sugar. And I lost thirty-five pounds. I stayed abstinent five years and maintained that weight loss. My confidence and self-esteem were great. I was on an OA honeymoon, receiving compliments and loving it.

> *I am, once again, doing everything I'm told. I don't ask questions; I just do it.*

And then the compliments stopped. About the same time, I stopped doing what I'd been told. I can't pinpoint the moment I went into relapse, but the warning signs were all there.

I was secretary of a meeting and my six-month term was up. I announced that it was time for me to step down, but no one volunteered to take over. It didn't occur to me to suggest that someone fill in on a week-to-week basis. I continued in the position, but inside I was grumbling, complaining, and judging all those people who didn't want to give service. Finally I simply announced that I was stepping down. Someone else took over, and I stopped coming to that meeting.

I also stopped using my sponsor. She was going through something at the time, and I felt she just wasn't there for me. I got another sponsor but would only call her once a week, and then just to chat. I still wasn't talking about what was really going on with me.

What was going on was the weight. I was justifying what I was eating and trying to control again. I went in for a physical and was horrified to learn that I'd gained fourteen pounds! This scared me but not enough to sit still, write about it, and talk to someone about what was happening.

On my birthday I gave myself permission to have a slice of cake. Soon I was having cake at everybody's birthday. I was in relapse and denial.

At an OA marathon, I heard a speaker talk about relapse. She said to share what you're going through, about the food you're having problems with, about the feelings, and especially about the shame. It dawned on me that I was in relapse – and ashamed to tell my OA friends about it.

My thinking was the worst it's ever been. While I didn't actually sit down and plan suicide, my thoughts were: "I can't go on this way," "I can't live this way," and "I can't face another day like this."

I finally started talking about my struggles with the weight, and the fact that I was eating binge foods again. I admitted that I had been in relapse for two years and had gained twenty-two pounds. In my relapse, I learned just how powerless I am over food – and that once a compulsive overeater, always a compulsive overeater.

Throughout my relapse, the one tool I kept using was meetings. I never stopped going. Now I see why the slogan, "Keep coming back," is so important! I also kept turning my will and my life over to God and praying for the willingness to be abstinent.

As I write this I've been abstinent two months. By the grace of God and OA, I've lost fourteen pounds. I attend both OA and OA-HOW meetings because I need the structure and discipline that I didn't have when I was in relapse.

I am, once again, doing everything I'm told. I don't ask questions; I just do it. My sponsor has only been in program three months, but I've learned a lot from her. The fact that I've been in program seven and a half years doesn't get in the way, for I see that it's quality, not quantity, that counts. I no longer think that I have all the answers. I don't want to do it my way anymore.

My relapse is part of my recovery. I must try to remember: I didn't lose my abstinence; I gave it away. I hope my story will help someone else who's going through a similar situation.

— *California USA*

Hungry. Angry. Lonely. Tired.

How did I fall into relapse? Simply put, I forgot I was a compulsive overeater. I've been in OA for many years, known as a long-timer by many members, yet I do not have all the answers. I knew the program, but was unable to work it as I became tired and immobilized from a very demanding job. But I was attending meetings regularly! It still can happen to members in OA. It is very comforting to know I am always welcome at meetings. "Keep coming back" reminds me of the open arms, support, and understanding from others who have experienced similar highs and lows.

I still have problems with cravings for food, although I still attend meetings and use some of the tools of recovery. I no longer belittle myself for my relapse; I know I'm doing the best I can right now. My willingness is growing, motivating me to use the rest of the tools. Willingness is a prerequisite to abstinence. Today I know abstinence and recovery are the most important things in my life. I don't function well at home or at work without them. By re-prioritizing my needs, I created the following list:

- Maintaining Higher Power contact
- Focusing on abstinence and recovery
- Being aware of my health
- Practicing a workable fitness program
- Being honest and lovingly tactful in my relationships
- Developing my special skills, talents, and gifts in my career

- Setting limits around workaholism

- Making quality time for my niece and nephew

- Scheduling fun time for myself.

Unfortunately, the work addiction had consumed all my other goals and priorities. HALT – Hungry, Angry, Lonely, Tired – quickly became my first awareness of relapse. I was exceedingly tired, all the time. I also realized how fast my "patience tank" was evaporating. I became easily agitated due to lack of sleep. Emotionally, my program was teetering, because I was simply too tired to attend meetings. Rest had become my priority.

I had no one to help me with the incredible demands of my business. Today I am looking for a new job and have reduced my overtime hours to a half-day a week only. I am trying to revive my energies physically, emotionally, and spiritually.

> *My willingness must now push me to reach out and call other compulsive eaters when the cravings start.*

My next step of willingness was to review all the tools to see which ones I was not using. I was going to meetings. I had a sponsor. I was reading my literature and using anonymity at meetings. I was writing in my journal. But I was not following a plan of eating. I was not doing service. I was not making phone calls.

I had to re-evaluate my relationship with my Higher Power. I was not praying in the morning before work. I was not taking the first three Steps every day. I'd let go of reading my daily meditation book. I saw that I needed to ask my Higher Power for help every morning to make it through the day. It had worked before: I knew that "God could and would if He were sought."

I had to think deeply about which Step I had last worked. Now, through this relapse, I acknowledge I am a compulsive overeater who is powerless over food (Step One). I know my Higher Power will restore me to sanity and help me (Step Two).

My willingness must now push me to reach out and call other compulsive eaters when the cravings start. I now understand that abstinence begins with an abstinent state of mind.

I've had to address impatience and non-acceptance of others in order to achieve an abstinent state of mind. Without working on these defects, I knew that I couldn't hold onto any length of abstinence. When my mind is truly abstinent, the rest of the program is so much easier. I've renewed my program by working those "lost" tools and Steps. I've managed to attend another meeting during the week with the reduction of overtime, and I'm doing more service work. I feel as if I'm a part of OA again, and that I'm helping to keep OA alive. I thank all of you in OA for being there and for keeping me alive.

— *Illinois USA*

Multiple Miracle

I came into OA out of pure desperation. I was on a tremendous amount of medication for high blood pressure and pain and needed a cane to walk. It was April of 1989, I was just about to turn thirty-six, and I weighed 350 pounds. Since the age of nineteen I hadn't been under 300 pounds except once, in preparation for my son's bar mitzvah, when I managed to get down to 280.

The first year in program I found acceptance, support, understanding and, most important, my abstinence. I lost 120 pounds. All of a sudden I had a life – free of medication and relatively free of pain. Little things that most people take for granted – walking briskly, sitting comfortably, and getting up from a chair gracefully – were finally within my reach. It was a miracle, and it was my miracle. With the help of four or five OA meetings and two therapy sessions a week, I was getting better emotionally, too. But my spirituality was still nonexistent.

I'd never been a drinker. Marijuana had always been my second escape route after food. Nonetheless, during the summer of 1990, I picked up alcohol and realized how much I liked it.

Without any knowledge or warning, I switched addictions. I

wouldn't smoke pot anymore because I knew I'd eat my brains out, but I was off and running with booze, believing I could keep food under control. Before I knew it, I was drinking day and night. I began backing away from OA meetings, and my food started getting sloppy.

In June of 1991, with the help of AA and my therapist, I stopped drinking. But putting down the food was a slower process. I'd been in full-blown relapse for months – totally out of control. The guilt, shame, and emotional pain were overwhelming, but I couldn't stop. My eating escalated to heights I didn't think possible, and I gained ninety pounds. I was right back where I started, the self-hatred more intense than ever before.

Why did this happen? Because I'm a compulsive overeater. How did it happen? I let people, places, and things cloud my judgment. I stopped taking care of me.

Another reason for my relapse: I was dissatisfied with my accomplishments in OA. I wasn't yet willing to surrender. I was impatient; the numbers on the scale were far too important. I was unable to accept a Higher Power, had nothing to fall back on and no one to guide me. Once again, I was petrified and desperate.

I never completely stopped going to meetings but was so embarrassed by my weight gain that I only went where nobody knew me. Finally I mustered the courage to start going to my old meetings. Instantly I knew the only one judging and ridiculing me was me.

July 30, 1991 would have been my dad's sixtieth birthday. In the morning I went to a meeting where I'd committed to attending thirty meetings in thirty days and, afterward, went to visit his grave. The tears came freely and lovingly, with no resentment or hostility. For the first time in eight years I was able to let go of guilt and just feel sad. My father was gone, and I missed him.

That night I cried out uncontrollably to God and surrendered my will. I admitted I was powerless and couldn't do it alone, and I begged for help. I got my abstinence and my life back. It hasn't been a perfect abstinence, but I'm not a perfect person, and I don't want to be. The pedestal is too high, and the fall far too painful.

I live my life one day at a time, and I work my program to the best of my ability. There are certain foods I don't eat. The compulsion to overeat has been lifted, and I strongly believe that God is doing for me what I cannot do for myself.

It's been almost a year, and I've taken off the ninety pounds – but I remember that pain. I have multiple addictions, each one interacting with the other, each one equally fatal. God willing, I won't forget, and I won't ever have to go back.

Once I became willing to turn my will over to my Higher Power, it became easier to start accepting and trusting myself. At times I still struggle with fear, doubt, and insecurity, but I have real freedom, too. I know that I have a disease which I can't control. My overeating isn't a moral issue anymore, so much of the shame I felt is gone.

It's a wonderful gift to look in the mirror and like who I see. I have faith in myself and believe that my Higher Power will take care of me when I don't think I can take care of myself.

Relapse is painful and devastating. I pray every day that I won't go through it again. But I'm grateful for the experience I did have. Without it, I wouldn't have the recovery I do today.

— *Massachusetts USA*

"Hold On! Don't Give Up!"

When I came into program a little over four years ago, I was hopeless. Not only with the food, but with everything! I just wanted to die. I thank God I was given the gift of OA, because that was where I finally found hope. I also found that I was not alone anymore.

For a while I continued to feel alone, and I struggled with the program. However, I did something I never had done in my whole life – I kept coming back. Still to this day, I live with these words.

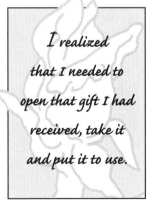

I realized that I needed to open that gift I had received, take it and put it to use.

My attitude had been, "If something doesn't work quickly enough, why bother?" I gave up on myself easily, and so did everyone around me. I just floated around on my little cloud going from place to place but never really staying anywhere. Every now and then I would land somewhere and gather bits and pieces of recovery, but I still would not stay. It just validated my own stupidity to me. "I am a helpless, hopeless, lost soul," I convinced myself.

Even coming into the OA meeting rooms, I felt that I would never get "the program." I kept getting back into the food. I kept trying to figure out what was wrong with me. I kept suggesting to myself that I needed other solutions: more professional treatment, more intense therapy, a change of environment, someone special in my life. All my life I had searched for something, and finally I was given that gift which was the program. But even in the meeting rooms of OA, I was still trying to search for something else. I realized, finally, that I could not do that anymore. I realized that I needed to open that gift I had received, take it and put it to use. I also needed to thank God, and return the favor by letting Him in and letting Him help me with the food and everything else in my life.

It has not been easy, but it has been worth the effort. I still want things to happen overnight. I still get in the selfish mode that I should be further in my journey. I'm learning that growth is a slow process; everything happens in God's time, not mine. What a concept!

It is a miracle to me that I kept coming back and haven't given up. When I first came into the program, I tried to keep in mind that all I needed to do was hold on and not give up. Some days, that was all I could do – just hold on and nothing else. Today I know that I'm only one bite away, and taking that bite will lead into that hopeless and isolated place I once lived. With program and God, I have hope, and with that hope I have the help not to give up on myself. Every day I have a choice to open the gift of recovery.

— *Pennsylvania USA*

Living the Solution

As encouraged by the World Service Business Conference, many of the meetings in our intergroup are holding a Twelfth-Step-Within meeting once a month. When I lead on the topic this week, I want to focus on the recovery from relapse, rather than why we are in relapse or why some of us continue to struggle after several years in the program. I'm keeping in mind that when I am not working my program as best I can, I allow myself to continue to be a slave to compulsive overeating.

Some questions I've had to ask myself are:

Am I truly committed to working this program? This means more than quickly reading *For Today* or fitting a meeting into my schedule. It means applying everything I've learned in the program to all aspects of my life.

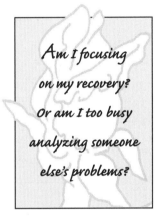

Am I focusing on my recovery? Or am I too busy analyzing someone else's problems?

Am I willing to get to a meeting, no matter what? Do I fit meetings into my schedule or work my schedule around the meetings? My program must come first in order for me to recover.

When I attend a meeting, am I of service? Am I willing to lead and set up the literature table, or do I arrive late and bolt out the door as soon as the meeting ends? Any service I perform at a meeting not only keeps the group healthy, but keeps me on the road to recovery.

When I share at a meeting, do I dump my problems, or am I an example of hope? Each of us has problems we need to share, but I can get stuck in the problem if I'm not looking to the solution.

Am I using Step Three? Am I hanging on to my problems, or am I turning them over to a Higher Power? Even though I never gave up a problem that didn't have claw marks on it, no problem has ever been solved by my worrying about it. Worry prevents recovery.

Do I have a sponsor? Am I willing to be a sponsor? Sponsors

help us work the Steps into recovery. Am I using my sponsor's experience or just chatting about the weather? Am I helping newcomers to understand their powerlessness?

Most important, am I focusing on my recovery? Or am I too busy analyzing someone else's problems? I cannot solve anyone else's problems, especially if they haven't asked for my input. The only way I am going to recover is to remember that I have choices. By putting my recovery first, I live in the solution.

I try to put the focus on recovery rather than relapse, because emphasizing relapse keeps me living the problem. Focusing on recovery and taking action is living the solution.

— *Illinois USA*

To the Care of God

Food never makes any situation better; it doesn't work for me anymore.

When I am in the turmoil of a dilemma, I need to rely on God, for in God is all truth, all power, and all the answers.

What would God have me say or do? I can't hear God's answer unless I get quiet, get centered, and listen to that still, small voice inside.

Sometimes my stress is so great that the roar of my emotions drowns God out. So I need to access my family: get to a meeting, call my sponsor, call another OA member, and talk about it. I need to use my OA tools, because I come from using food to cope. The truth is that, at times of disturbance, to remain in recovery I must seek help from a Power greater than myself.

Thirteen years' experience in OA has also taught me that God works through people. And we – God and I, therefore you and I – can do what I cannot.

Of course, I don't always remember to do this perfectly. But the solution is always there. It's up to me to take the appropriate action of considering my options and, in so doing, seeking God's help.

One thing I do know from many years of practicing this disease before OA and yo-yoing between relapse and recovery in OA: food never makes any situation better; it doesn't work for me anymore. It hasn't for four and a half years of abstinence. And God's grace allows me to maintain a 168-pound weight loss! Food is still an option, but not a viable one, just for today.

I must rely on this Power greater than myself because my very life depends on it. I need God's strength, help, and truth. I need to believe I'm God's child, and God will be there no matter what. I don't have to be good or behave or be perfect to deserve love, guidance, care, and abundance. All I have to do is be.

I'm feeling confused and overwhelmed facing a major decision in my life. And I'm willing to go to any length to respect myself by abstaining and doing whatever God would have me do to live my life in recovery. Certainly the footwork is up to me, but the results and the miracles are God's job.

— *California USA*

Seven Years and Counting

I went to my first OA meeting in February 1985 because I was five feet, two and a half inches tall and weighed 285 pounds. I knew it wouldn't take much to get to three hundred pounds, and I was terrified.

I didn't believe I was a compulsive overeater – but I did keep coming back.

I remember listening to those who shared at that first meeting and thinking that I didn't belong there. People were talking about feelings, and I was there for a diet. By meeting's end, I'd already decided that OA was not for me. Then someone came over to me and told me not to judge the program by this one meeting and to keep coming back. God bless that person.

Week after week, I kept coming back. I didn't comprehend the

Steps, didn't use the tools, didn't understand abstinence, and didn't believe I was a compulsive overeater – but I did keep coming back. Slowly I began sharing.

After one year it occurred to me to ask someone to sponsor me. I was ready to work my program. I'd lost over 135 pounds. How? I wrote, read, meditated, did service, and went to meetings.

A lot of time and effort has gone into my program since those first years. And yet, five years into the program, I remember being afraid that I wouldn't keep the weight off. I'd read statistics that said obese people tend to gain all their weight back after five years. When I confided this new fear to my sponsor, she told me that statistics hadn't been gathered for formerly obese people who are abstinent, attending meetings, calling their sponsors, sponsoring others, giving service, and so forth. My sponsor is right. In the. "Big Book" it says that if I continue to do what I'm doing today, I will not pick up the food.

For today I work my program the best way I know how. I am maintaining my weight loss and have a miraculously wonderful life. I continue to give hope to those who knew me "when" and those who know me now.

— *New York USA*

The Twelve Steps of Overeaters Anonymous

1. We admitted we were powerless over food – that our lives had become unmanageable.

2. Came to believe that a Power greater than ourselves could restore us to sanity.

3. Made a decision to turn our will and our lives over to the care of God *as we understood Him.*

4. Made a searching and fearless moral inventory of ourselves.

5. Admitted to God, to ourselves, and to another human being the exact nature of our wrongs.

6. Were entirely ready to have God remove all these defects of character.

7. Humbly asked Him to remove our shortcomings.

8. Made a list of all persons we had harmed and became willing to make amends to them all.

9. Made direct amends to such people wherever possible, except when to do so would injure them or others.

10. Continued to take personal inventory and when we were wrong, promptly admitted it.

11. Sought through prayer and meditation to improve our conscious contact with God *as we understood Him,* praying only for knowledge of His will for us and the power to carry that out.

12. Having had a spiritual awakening as the result of these Steps, we tried to carry this message to compulsive overeaters and to practice these principles in all our affairs.

Permission to use the Twelve Steps of Alcoholics Anonymous for adaptation granted by AA World Services, Inc.

The Twelve Traditions of Overeaters Anonymous

1. Our common welfare should come first; personal recovery depends upon OA unity.

2. For our group purpose there is but one ultimate authority – a loving God as He may express Himself in our group conscience. Our leaders are but trusted servants; they do not govern.

3. The only requirement for OA membership is a desire to stop eating compulsively.

4. Each group should be autonomous except in matters affecting other groups or OA as a whole.

5. Each group has but one primary purpose – to carry its message to the compulsive overeater who still suffers.

6. An OA group ought never endorse, finance, or lend the OA name to any related facility or outside enterprise, lest problems of money, property, and prestige divert us from our primary purpose.

7. Every OA group ought to be fully self-supporting, declining outside contributions.

8. Overeaters Anonymous should remain forever nonprofessional, but our service centers may employ special workers.

9. OA, as such, ought never be organized; but we may create service boards or committees directly responsible to those they serve.

10. Overeaters Anonymous has no opinion on outside issues; hence the OA name ought never be drawn into public controversy.

11. Our public relations policy is based on attraction rather than promotion; we need always maintain personal anonymity at the level of press, radio, films, television, and other public media of communication.

12. Anonymity is the spiritual foundation of all these Traditions, ever reminding us to place principles before personalities.

Permission to use the Twelve Traditions of Alcoholics Anonymous for adaptation granted by AA World Services, Inc.

For more information on Overeaters Anonymous or for a copy of OA's literature catalog, write the World Service Office, P.O. Box 44020, Rio Rancho, New Mexico 87174-4020, or call (505) 891-2664.